MW00928347

Win
the Day

How to win your battles with
stress, anxiety & depression

by John Cunningham

Copyright © 2021 John Cunningham

All rights reserved.
No part of this book may be reproduced or used in any manner without written
permission of the copyright owner except for the use of quotations in a book review.

ISBN: 978-1-7374747-4-6

JC Press
San Jose, CA

Cover and Interior layout design by Tami Boyce (tamiboyce.com)

I dedicate this book to you, my reader.

Maintaining good mental health is not easy.
I am eternally grateful to you for choosing this book
as a resource to help you fight those battles.

Disclaimers:

Use of quotes and mentions of people in this book does not in any way express or imply their endorsement of this book or its contents. Likewise, mentions of products or services is not an endorsement of those.

I am not a medical professional, the advice given in this book has worked for me. There is no guarantee expressed or implied that it will work for you. If you are having mental health issues that are beyond your ability to cope with, please seek out professional assistance.

Table of Contents

Introduction

$\mathcal{J}$ ames and his friends Peter and Maria had climbed three-quarters of the way up the nearly 10,000 foot (2,999 meters) sheer north face of Cima Grande (The Grand Chimney) in Italy's Dolomite Mountains. Suddenly a cloudburst made the steep face of the chimney appear unsaleable. As they held on for dear life, the three friends needed to make a decision. Would they wait out the rain and continue to the summit or descend the rock and hope for another opportunity to scale it in a day or two before heading back home?

Maria suggested that they had not come this far to let a little rain stop them. Once it passed, they could continue on and reach the peak. After all, they prepared for a month back home in Colorado for these climbs. This one was the most difficult part of their trip and would be the pinnacle achievement of their experiences in Italy if they completed it. They had already successfully scaled Cima Piccola and Cima Ovest on their adventure. Peter had doubts about whether the wet rocks and extremely narrow paths would be safe to continue climbing. He also worried about the descent, which seemed more treacherous than the ascent. Having torn off his fingernail earlier in the day, Peter firmly believed that retreat was the best solution. James, though exhausted, felt determined to keep going even though he slipped and nearly plunged several meters twice on the climb. He was feeling every ache and pain from those mishaps and the previous days of intense climbing. That did not keep him from his burning desire for success. A protein bar or two and some water, he thought, will sustain me, enabling us to summit.

Once the rain stopped, they began to climb again. One small, seemingly insignificant advance, then another. Before too much longer, what at one time seemed like an insurmountable task now appeared achievable. One decision and one maneuver at a time, they continued. Collectively, they found the strength to carry on and succeed in their quest to get to the peak, conquering the Dolomites.

Sitting at the top of the world in silence, each of them considered what this trip meant to them. They had conquered individual fears and moments when defeat seemed imminent. Yet, they worked as a team to achieve what seemed impossible just a short time before. Then, as they celebrated together, they shared a collective smile, knowing that they will each carry this experience with them for the rest of their lives. A bond they will always share.

Life is a lot like that. When facing challenges and opportunities which provide chances to make strides in life, we are often called upon to trust in ourselves, those around us, and accept challenges that are unexpected and often scary. These difficulties may require you to use all your skills, strengths, and knowledge to meet them. Once you have conquered those obstacles, you will forever know that you can achieve more than you initially thought was possible.

Like James, nearly falling a few times before summiting, setbacks are inevitable in life. No one makes the right decision every time. Instead, it's how we transcend those failures and prepare to succeed the next time that is the difference. We can plan for the risks and mitigating factors, then take measures to account for those. Ultimately, we need to have faith in ourselves to achieve progress in life, regardless of the circumstances. The mantra of progress, not perfection, should drive us.

That is what *Win the Day* is all about. Presenting tools and systems that enable you to challenge life's difficulties day in, day out, and eventually overcome them. Through this book, you will learn to become more confident in yourself by discovering a deeper purpose in your life. You will develop techniques and grasp principles that allow you to win your daily struggles with stress, anxiety, and depression. I know these concepts work because I have used every idea in this book to become a more fulfilled, positive, and successful person. They are neither difficult nor above your skill level. Anyone and everyone can successfully apply these techniques and processes. Adopt what you learn in this book, and you can become braver in the face of your fears, more accepting of yourself and others, and in tune with the world around you.

Good mental health is one of the greatest challenges many of us face, unfortunately talking about this part of life carries some stigma. Regardless of its causes, implementing steps to take more control of your life now and in the future is something you can do every day. Just like Maria, Peter and James found great satisfaction in their lives by achieving their goals one decision and maneuver at a time, step by step you too can have a life of which you feel proud. You deserve that. Win the day today, and you will be better equipped to manage your tomorrows.

You

*I*n this first part of *Win the Day,* I focus on you. You are the starting point for everything that follows. To begin with, you must accept yourself as you are. You are a gift and you have so many reasons to be right here, right now. Get ready to walk into a more confident and successful life. Then as you build a deeper relationship with yourself, you will need to let love into your life. Love is both a powerful feeling and a powerful state of being, and to share it you first must possess it. Loving yourself allows you to find the beauty in who you are regardless of scars, regrets or faults. Finding love for yourself will raise your confidence and allow you to present yourself the gifts of forgiveness, grace and dignity. Nobody is perfect, but that shouldn't keep you from striving to become the best possible version of yourself. This is why I wrote the book you hold now in your hands, to help you become the person that your mind's eye can see, even if you don't know how to get there, yet.

When you can forgive yourself for your errors and embrace the miracle that you are, you'll begin to see that you are being primed for something bigger, something better, so long as you are up for the challenge. And if you're not, at least you can find a way to be deeply satisfied with the person you spend more time with than any other, you.

Once your loving relationship with yourself grows and expands, it will be time to relate and share that with the world around you. You are not alone. In fact, you are interconnected to the entire universe. Finding or rediscovering that spiritual connection, *however you define it*, will help you have a clearer perspective on your purpose in the world and your ability to fulfill it. Taking complete responsibility for your life and your circumstances from this day forward is vital if you want not only to win the day, but win the rest of your life too.

Finally, becoming a better version of yourself and winning the battles over stress, anxiety and depression is not something you do once, and it's over and forever achieved. Life will always present new challenges, lingering memories and recurring issues. Being all in on yourself and your life will allow you to gain confidence, self-respect and a sense of purpose that is uniquely yours. These are the first tools you will need if you are going to attain the life you're capable of, the life you deserve.

1. Believe in Yourself

*R*obert had a dream. He wanted to write for the *Washington Post*. His friends and family thought he was crazy. He always got C's in English, and despite his best efforts, one of his high school teachers told him he would never be a good writer.

Still, Robert remained determined. He started writing a blog and over time his writing improved. Robert wrote content for people who were building their own websites. He even started writing stories on *Medium*, a site for both aspiring and accomplished writers.

Robert found some success writing for himself and submitting articles about his other hobbies, classic car restoration and photography, to niche websites and publications. He decided it was time to raise the bar. He sent an opinion piece to the *Washington Post* about the need for high schools to include more practical subjects like auto shop and personal finance in their curriculum. To his surprise, they published it. Robert didn't stop there. He had experienced some of the satisfaction he sought, but had not yet accomplished his dream of being a regular contributor.

He continued to write and improve his craft by studying on his own and writing for others through contests and winning contracts on freelance sites like Fiverr. Then one day it happened. He saw a commission from *the WAPO* asking for an article on a classic car show in his hometown. He submitted a response with three articles he had written about classic cars and the nostalgic vehicle lifestyle. Not only did he win that commission, but it was so well received that he continued to get offers to write for other newspapers, magazines and websites all around the world. None of this would have been possible if Robert hadn't believed in himself and continued to pursue his ambitions regardless of what others told him.

You can find success in your life, too. It starts with believing in yourself above all others and developing a mindset that you can achieve what you envision for your life.

> *If you believe in yourself and have dedication and pride - and never quit, you'll be a winner. The price of victory is high but so are the rewards.*
>
> —Bear Bryant

Life Is Not Stacked Against You

When life feels like everything is against you, it's not uncommon to seek support and comfort in the words of others, like a warm blanket. However comforting it may seem to blame the world or accredit something that doesn't go well to bad luck, that won't help you get where you want to go. You need to have faith that you can achieve the success you dream of. No one else can do it for you. Like Robert, you need to walk down a path on your own making.

When you feel overwhelmed, instead of saying, "I have a problem," try changing your point of view with an expression like, "I have a challenge." This will help you to believe that you can surmount any obstacle and achieve your goals.

I see problems as opportunities. When things don't go as planned or a complex situation is dropped in my lap, I consider what I am supposed to learn from the experience and what I have learned before that I can apply to this quagmire. Many times, I have seen a present challenge turn into an opportunity later.

It's all about mindset. I am sure that's true for you too. What is something that at first seemed like a problem or enigma that was too big for you, but later you found that it prepared you for another opportunity? When you can identify benefits from the struggle, you will look at each challenge as an opportunity to grow; even short-term failures will take you further down the path to success than you are today.

Win Life One Day at a Time

You can look back in dismay at all the could'ves, would'ves and should'ves; but we both know that won't get you very far. You can accept the words of others over belief in yourself, or you can choose to find one small thing to do today that will move you closer to the vision you have of your tomorrows. When you decide to live with a belief that no matter what difficulties you face you will overcome them, you are becoming a more complete person every day. You build your ability to take on the challenges and get through them. Instead of putting off that task until tomorrow or picking at it, hoping it will go away, take action—the bigger and more dynamic the better. Deciding to live with the belief that no matter what difficulties you face, you shall become a more polished version of yourself every day is something you *should* do right now.

What life-changing challenge you have been avoiding? What is one thing you can do today that will move you towards victory over it?

> *You have to believe in yourself when no one else does -*
> *that makes you a winner right there.*
>
> —*Venus Williams*

Self-Respect NOT Self-Reject

It is easy to find the many things you have done wrong in your life, to relive the times you have fallen short or others have criticized you for one reason or another. Stop doing that! Stop dwelling on the negative. Stop giving the past so much space in your life today. Take a deep breath of fresh and more fulfilling experiences. Focus on the positive, because life is about progress. When you find yourself dwelling on the past, breathe in, breathe out, and accept that the past is behind you. Do what you can to release your feelings of regret. I have made many mistakes in my life but I do not regret a single one of them because I cannot change the past and everything that has happened in my life, whether as the result of my intents and purposes or those of another, have led to my growth into the person that I am now.

Take what you have learned in life, your experiences and your accomplishments and use those experiences as you move forward.

They will help you to make today better than yesterday. That will make tomorrow better, too. I can't remember all my failures, there have been far too many to count. Yet, I would not take one do-over. Those experiences have brought me to where I am now. I believe that if anything would have gone differently, I would also be different. Maybe I would have never earned a black belt, lived in Japan or written this book. So, I am grateful for those blunders. You should be too. If you have failed, learn from it. If you have succeeded, consider how you could do more or get even better results next time. Never settle, you deserve more.

Be Kind to Yourself

Life is a war, and you need to win it battle by battle. To do so, it is important to recognize that your path is unique and the campaigns you encounter will be different from those others are fighting. Don't expect to win your life by constantly comparing yourself to others, belittling yourself or finding fault with what you do. Instead, give yourself compassion and a pat on the back for facing the conflicts, challenges and decisions that comprise your daily existence, even when you don't win them all. Because you won't.

You may long for the days when there are no difficulties and life seems like a walk on the beach, or every hour is happy hour. That is not reality. Instead, take comfort in your efforts, knowing that, in the long run, you are making your life better.

Though situations may seem worse today than they were yesterday, it will not always be that way. Diligently create a better tomorrow. Stick with it, make progress a little at a time, and look for signs that you are moving in the right direction. That is how you will truly be kind to yourself, by working towards a better version of yourself.

One way that I recognize the victories is to write a weekly to-do list. As I cross tasks off the list and reflect on what I've completed at the end of each day, I realize that I have accomplished far more than I had thought. This *I did* list may help you count your victories too.

Don't Take S*** From Anyone

Billy Joel ends his concerts by telling his fans, "Don't take shit from anyone!" You shouldn't either. Most other people don't know your innermost desires, what you can achieve and the road you have traveled. In fact, others often view your life from their own perspectives, thinking you are just like them. You are not. You have your own mission in life, and provided that it is non-destructive, you owe it to yourself to pursue that.

You have your own gifts to give. As you are growing your talents and abilities, continue to build that inner faith and self-belief that will help you to close your ears to destructive criticism. Developing this tough skin will allow you to grow like a maple tree, full of promise with the strength to weather storms. You can achieve what your mind perceives. You just need to balance the grind and hard work of growth with acceptance and care for the wonderful person that you are.

Promise me you'll always remember: You're braver than you believe, and stronger than you seem, and smarter than you think.

—*A. A. Milne*

You've Got to Believe

No one else can live your life. That job is already taken. No one else can achieve your purpose, that gift was given to you alone. Despite what has happened in your life before or what you have done, you can shape your future. If you haven't done so already, start down that path today.

You have a life of purpose and are capable of making beneficial contributions. You owe it to yourself to live a life you can be proud of—believe in yourself. This may seem like an impossible mission, but it is not. All it takes is little steps and making improvement over time. Slow and steady wins the race.

Don't worry about your past, that's done. Accept the challenge of becoming the best version of yourself, and do it today. There will be backsliding, no question about it. Nevertheless, when you look back on where you have been and how you have grown a month, a year or even several years later, you will be proud of the commitment you have made to yourself and the battles you've fought. Accept the challenges in your life as learning experiences, knowing in your heart of hearts that you were born to win.

Seeing Is Believing

One way to build belief in yourself is to keep *I can*, and *I did* lists. Your *I can* list is one that includes the things you do well. If you are not sure of what those things are, ask three trustworthy friends to list your strengths and examples of how you've done those. Put your accomplishments front and center. Then look at this list when you feel you are not progressing or feeling down.

Use your *I did* list to note your daily accomplishments. Then review the list at the end of the day, week and month. During weeks I feel I made little progress, my *I did* list blows me away. It is hard to believe all the little battles I've won. Likewise, for you the trudging days or weeks may be times you make the greatest progress in your journey. By getting these accomplishments out of your head and in front of your eyes, it will allow you to have a clearer understanding of the movement you are making towards your goals and aspirations. Seeing is believing.

> *Faith that it's not always in your hands or things don't always go the way you planned, but you have to have faith that there is a plan for you, and you must follow your heart and believe in yourself no matter what.*
>
> —Martina McBride

Tying It All Together

No one knows you the way you do, so be careful of what thoughts and words you let in. You have a divine purpose. As you live that, many people will come into your life that are generally supportive. There will also be others that only want to drag you down. Have faith in yourself and rise above the muck to become the person you were meant to be. It will not be easy, and you may feel like you are failing at times. However, by taking life a day at a time and picking up victories, little victories along the way, you will find your path to a more fulfilling life than you could have previously imagined. When times are tough, believe in yourself.

Here are some exercises to help you enhance your belief in yourself

▶ Reframe problems as challenges. Challenges provide an opportunity to grow while problems are burdens.

▶ Write down three challenges and the benefits of solving them.

▶ What is something that at first seemed like a problem or challenge which was too big for you, but later you discovered that it prepared you for another opportunity?

▶ What is a potential life changing challenge you have been avoiding?
  ▷ What are some actions you can do to move closer to clearing that challenge?

▶ Write an "I did" list. Tasks you intend to complete during the week (you can add to this list as the week continues).
  ▷ Cross off the tasks as you achieve them.

▶ Write an "I can" list. Things you can do that have a positive impact on your life and the world around you.

Get your free companion workbook for additional support at https://www.synergypersonaldevelopment.com/workbook/

2. The First Love Is Self-Love

*M*ainstream media has created images of life that are difficult, if not impossible, for us to compete with: slim and muscular bodies, rich and carefree lifestyles, and ultra-compassionate characters who never get angry. This leaves most of us feeling inadequate. Piling on top of those feelings of inadequacy are experiences like losing a job, ending a relationship, or struggling to gain a new talent. All these experiences can lead to feelings of disillusionment. To combat that negative self-talk, you need to believe there is something special in you and about you. Have faith in yourself and learn to love the person inside.

You Can't Give What You Don't Have

To love yourself is to accept who you are, despite your flaws and inadequacies. Loving yourself means you are comfortable spending time alone, and that you are your own biggest fan regardless of the circumstances. Over a lifetime you will spend many more years with yourself than any friend, partner or family member. You will know all the secrets, all the sacrifices and all the dashed dreams. You will know the hard work that went into your accomplishments and the lesson learned from your failures. Love and be happy with the person you see in the mirror. Love yourself and your world will blossom.

Relying on others for your feeling of self-worth is dangerous, because not all the people around you have your best interest at heart. In actuality, many have their own agendas. Their plans are independent of and sometimes in direct conflict with yours. Seeking praise from those who secretly scorn you will only provide short-lived satisfaction as you work to help them achieve their schemes. However, appreciating yourself and your accomplishments and spending time around people who genuinely value you will feed your self-confidence, and help you to distance yourself from victim's mentality.

Learn to accept the person you are, with all your faults and frailties. Finding peace with yourself allows you to be an authentic contributor to your own life and establishes a sense of accountability to yourself. If there is something you don't like, change it. If you are unsatisfied with the quality of your efforts, experiment with ways that can help you perform better. Having a deep sense of love and appreciation for yourself allows you to know what you're capable of and increases your level of personal commitment. Only you know you how far you can push yourself, and it's probably further than you think. Reaching further and finding success leads to an enhanced sense of pride. When you have the confidence that comes with being content with yourself, you see others for the valuable people they are as well.

A vital ingredient to a deeper sense of self love is self-esteem. When you feel good in your own skin, you can readily accept the world around you. Self-esteem doesn't mean you need to feel that you are superior to others. It's more about being comfortable with who you are. This comfort allows you to authentically engage in your environment. Start with eye-to-eye affirmations in the mirror. Tell yourself, "I love you" and "I'm glad to be me." These proclamations will help you feel a deep sense of self-worth. Soon you will come to accept that you cannot trade your situation for someone else's. Eventually, you will not want to trade your circumstances for another's. Over time, you will enjoy being who you are and embracing the opportunities in front of you. Get busy fighting your good fight, you deserve it.

> *I think the most important thing in life is self-love, because if you don't have self-love, and respect for everything about your own body, your own soul, your own capsule, then how can you have an authentic relationship with anyone else?*
>
> *—Shailene Woodley*

It is said that you cannot give what you don't have. And so, to give honest, deep and sincere love to others, you need to start by giving and receiving it from yourself. That starts with self-respect, then developing trust, and finally bringing a sense of joy to being who you are. Developing self-love will create harmony within you. If your environment is healthy, this good feeling will be mirrored and magnified by your surroundings. Conversely, if your environment seems to be filled with conflict and negativity, this may be a sign that you need more enriching surroundings.

When you have self-love, you will enjoy your life more, be more supportive, cooperative, and interested in others. Along with yourself, you will want others to flourish for their own benefit, with no hidden agendas. As you develop feelings of love and respect for yourself, start holding yourself more accountable to your own expectations rather than those placed on you by others. Expect to give your best effort every time, win or lose. Love is not always soft. Often taking on a challenge leads you to a better version of who you are. Through these trials you learn to be true to yourself, your beliefs and your principles.

To gain a deeper understanding of your likes and dislikes, your preferences and your distinct tastes, make a list of places, activities and thing you love and abhor and why. Expressing your reasons for these strong dispositions will allow you to specify the experiences you want in your life and help you to discover ways to manifest those regularly. As you realize these partialities, you can actively seek out the positive and joyful ones, leading to increasingly authentic and fulfilling experiences that help you to thrive.

Putting Yourself First Is an Act of Self-Love

We have been told since we were kids that putting yourself first is selfish. While those who do not have your best interests in mind may be put off by this approach to life, any assertion that it is selfish couldn't be further from the truth. If you are going to give your best, you need to understand how to achieve your best. What environment do you need? What tools? Focusing on your needs will help you serve others as well—like they say on the airplanes, put your own oxygen mask on first so that you can then help others. Just as it is important to create an environment that includes more of the things you have an affinity for, to achieve your best, you need to create the environment that supports you in doing so. It's not selfish at all, it's being responsible to yourself and those your actions serve.

> *Remember, if you ever need a helping hand, it's at the end of your arm, as you get older, remember you have another hand: The first is to help yourself, the second is to help others.*
>
> —*Audrey Hepburn*

Self-Love Vs. Narcissism

Those who consider putting themselves first a selfish act may be confusing self-love with narcissism. Self-love focuses on benevolence, creating harmony with your environment, and high levels of self-esteem. Someone who has self-love accepts themselves and others as they are. Possessing self-love allows you to be honest with yourself and those around you. If you have self-love, you are able to embrace all that you are and willing to share that version of yourself with the world.

A narcissist, conversely, thinks the world revolves around them. Everything and everyone is here to support the narcissists. They are self-centered and possess an exaggerated sense of self-importance. Narcissists are manipulative and secretive. Narcissist don't feel love in a deep and fulfilling way because they are too focused on how to get what they want from others and making themselves look good.

Developing love for yourself allows you to share it with others. But before you can give it, you need to possess love.

> *Self-love has very little to do with how you feel about your outer self. It's about accepting all of yourself.*
>
> —*Tyra Banks*

Tying It All Together

Developing self-love is challenging. It requires you to accept yourself completely with all your scars and imperfections—unconditional love. Start to develop love for yourself through positive affirmations and accepting your faults and liabilities. None of us is perfect, come to embrace that imperfection in yourself. Remember that others' opinions are judgements formed in their own minds, so filter those before taking them on-board. Give yourself some time to understand the real you, your likes, dislikes, strengths and weaknesses. Then you can create an environment that allows you to develop into the best version of yourself.

Here are some exercises to help you increase your self-love

- Every morning and evening for one week use these affirmations while looking in the mirror:
  - ▷ I love you
  - ▷ I'm glad to be me

To gain a deeper understanding of your likes and dislikes, your preferences and your distinct tastes:

- ▶ Make a list of places, activities and thing you love.
  - ▷ Why do you love those?

- ▶ Make a list of places, activities and thing you hate.
  - ▷ Why do you hate those?

Expressing your reasons for these strong dispositions will allow you to specify the experiences you want in your life and help you to discover ways to manifest those regularly.

- ▶ Answer the following questions about yourself, and explain your answers in as much detail as possible:
  - ▷ What is your favorite food?
    - ◆ Why?
  - ▷ Who is your favorite artist?
    - ◆ Why
  - ▷ Do you prefer coffee, tea or another beverage?
    - ◆ Why?
  - ▷ What is a place near you that you love to visit?
    - ◆ Why
  - ▷ What circumstances and surroundings allow you to do your best work?
    - ◆ How can you create that or a similar environment?

Get your free companion workbook for additional support at https://www.synergypersonaldevelopment.com/workbook/

3. Believe in Something Higher

*There is nothing that wastes the body like worry,
and one who has any faith in (something higher) should
be ashamed to worry about anything whatsoever.*

—Mahatma Gandhi

If you want to have the power to achieve more and make bigger contributions in your life, you have to be motivated by more than just yourself. You need to serve something higher. Your chosen spiritual source may be The Creator, Jesus, Nirvana, Muhammed, the Force or nature. There are no limits to sources of spiritual connection. Whatever it is, developing that sacred relationship allows you to create a deep bond to the world around you. For me, this bond provides a foundation of trust belief, and accountability. It also reduces my anxiety about the issues in life that are beyond my control.

Who or What Do You Serve?

Serving something bigger than yourself puts your life into perspective. It makes you feel connected to society and the world. It can also inspire you to keep creating and encourage others. You do your job and that brings financial rewards and hopefully a sense of fulfillment. That job is not the be all end all of your contribution to the world. Connecting to others outside your own clan allows you to comprehend the interconnectedness you have with this immense world. You'll more clearly understand how you serve, no matter what work you do and how you spend you available time. You are making a difference not just through direct contribution, but also the exponential benefits to those to whom you impact.

It does not matter what your religious or spiritual beliefs are. In fact, you do not have to believe in any deity at all. What is important is that you are serving something greater than yourself. This desire to serve a higher purpose is part of human's internal wiring. Tapping that hallowed energy will help you move into the future with more ambition during the highs, and a feeling of being cradled and supported as you work through the low points. Connecting in a deeper ethereal manner will help you to answer these questions:

▶ Why are you here?

▶ What are you meant to experience?

▶ What are you meant to achieve?

▶ What is the lesson in this struggle?

▸ Based on your knowledge, strength and experience, how are you to make a difference?

Having some answers to those, regardless of how substantial is beneficial to your peace of mind and building a firm foundation of who you are and what you want to achieve.

You're Not Alone

When you believe in something higher, you can feel that you are not alone. Often, we look for that in people who have had similar experiences. This support network can help you to make it through the loneliness and isolation you may feel as you reach and grow as a person. Living in a foreign country, I often find myself in solitude. I need a connection I can take with me anywhere and call on in any situation, so spiritual connection really helps.

Spiritual belief fuels a sense of meaning and purpose in my life. As you develop yours, you will see struggles as purposeful, and victories as more significant than they might be otherwise. This belief helps you to move beyond your egoic feelings to a co-contributor's mindset. I often start my days by meditating on how I am supposed to contribute today. This keeps me balanced and focused on achieving progress one day at a time. Doing this exercise will help you to build a stronger relationship with your higher source, and become more focused on the contributions your works make.

As the quote from Gandhi above expresses, when you have faith, you do not need worry. Everything that is put before you, serves a purpose. Take some time to deeply consider what that purpose is. Through this discovery you will grow as a person and that growth will propel you towards accomplishment. It is an endless cycle of reflection and discovery. Similarly, not taking the time to fully digest your life dilemmas and decisions will have you repeating the lessons again and again until you get the answers right. Don't try to avoid these; they serve as signposts for your life. If you are having problems with memories and thoughts you'd rather avoid, entertain these, meet them head on. When you face your fears, disappointments, and even horrors you will begin to gain control over them. Step by step you can put them to use, serving you to achieve a higher purpose in your life. This is much preferred to the alternative of those plaguing ideas consuming you. You are not alone, you are part of a higher power, no matter what you call it and whether or not you even believe it exists.

> *I think that anything that begins to give people*
> *a sense of their own worth and dignity is God.*
>
> —*John Shelby Spong*

Be brave in facing your fears, tragedies and regrets. That is the only way to unbind yourself from their chains. Trust that you are not alone is facing these, your god is with you. Supporting you in your healing and holding you when the grief appears too great. Believe that there is a great force driving you towards extraordinary achievement. It's not easy, but nothing worth achieving ever is.

Tying It All Together

Mary works in a supermarket. Every day she meets the same kinds of people, most of whom treat her and her coworkers with disdain. Every night she comes home tired and irritable. Until one day, having had enough of the negativity, she decides to take a novel approach.

She changes her mindset to considering that through her service, she herself is part of the team that helps these people feed their minds, bodies and families. She begins to smile at every customer. She takes an interest in their struggles and ends transactions with, "Thank you for choosing to shop in our store." Or "Looks like you will enjoy a satisfying meal tonight." She has not only changed her approach, but the shoppers' mindset too.

She has made a connection to serving the community and that in turn helps her to realize a contribution to society through her work. It has become more than just standing at a check stand scanning groceries and collecting money. Her work now has a transformational quality to it. She's imparting a dash of goodness and spreading some positive energy. That positive energy will also make her customers' ride home a bit more pleasant and their dinners taste a little better.

This positive shift is possible for you too, if you want it. It starts with considering what you are contributing and how you serve. If you aren't happy with your answers, start making some changes. Without a sense of contribution, a job is just something you are doing to make money. A family is just a group of people that keep you from your own interest, and community service is something you do because you feel some external obligation to do so.

With a sense of contribution, those things all take on a much deeper meaning. Believing that there is something beyond your physical world will help you feel that what you are working for is within your reach. It is achievable! If it weren't, you would not be visualizing it. Have the courage to act on your visions and reach for exponential growth. By aiming for the stars, you will go far.

Think higher, think deeper. The people you serve, the positivity you spread, the ripples you start are all things within your control. Belief in something beyond yourself will provide that ability.

Here is are some exercises to help you connect to a higher presence

- Read spiritual texts. Here are some to get you started:
  - ▷ *The Prophet* by Kahil Gibran
  - ▷ *Siddhartha* by Herman Hesse
  - ▷ *The Art of Happiness: A Handbook for Living* by the Dalai Lamma
  - ▷ *Illusions: The Adventures of a Reluctant Messiah* by Richard Bach
  - ▷ *The Four Agreements: A Practical Guide to Personal Freedom* by Don Miguel Ruiz

- Take a spiritual self-assessment by answering these questions:
  - ▷ Why are you here?
  - ▷ What are you meant to experience?
  - ▷ What are the lessons in that?
  - ▷ What are you meant to achieve?

▷ What is something you could do to step towards that achievement?

▷ What are some ways you serve the world beyond yourself and your family?

▷ Based on your knowledge, strengths and experiences, how can you make a difference in your community or on a larger scale?

Get your free companion workbook for additional support at https://www.synergypersonaldevelopment.com/workbook/

4. If You Want a Brighter Future, Release the Past

*P*oor Milena, it seems she is always worried that things won't go well for her because she had this or that unpleasant experience in the past. Milena often judges her friends based on their past actions.

A few years ago, Milena's friend, Paul, scratched her car. He opened the door quickly and accidentally hit it against a pole. Melina never lets him forget about that. She mentions the scratch every time Paul gets in her car. Another time Milena made a presentation and it did not go very well. Now she refuses to do them at all. One wonders how Milena can make any progress in her life or keep any friends when she is so focused on the past.

If you, like Milena, bear grudges, and continually visualize past negative experiences, it is time you stop living in the past and start focusing on creating a new future.

The Past Is Gone & It's Not Coming Back

Your past has gotten you to where you are today. It is a quilt of experiences and thoughts that have prepared you for this moment, but it is gone, never to return. The reason it's called his-story or her-story is that it has already been written. Nothing you can do or say will ever bring it back. The only choice you have now is to stay stuck while the world passes you by or to move forward.

The past can be a place of comfort. It gives you a reminder of what was, and clear expectations of how things will be in the future if you stay the course, no surprises or tough decisions, but no growth or adventure either. Regardless of whether the past is where your greatest accomplishments lie, or is a place of horror, it is behind you, and you need to release it.

Attempting to stay there is futile at best and dangerous at worst. Futile because the external factors such as your age, your experience and the people and conditions around you are different. Oftentimes, past traumatic experiences linger in the memory as continual suffering. While ideally we would leave the suffering behind, take the lessons from the past and move on, this is not always possible. If you can't escape these past situations on your own you it would be a good idea to seek professional help. There are valuable lessons to garner from previous experiences pertaining to both what to do and not do. The past is gone, the future is uncertain, all you really have is now. Focusing on and making changes in the now is the way to direct your future. That's the only way to win the day.

Pack Your Bags & Move On

Instead of dwelling on and in the past, chart your course and journey into the great unknown of your future. It doesn't pay to agonize over your past mistakes, or to live in the might have beens. These thoughts will only fill your mind with grief, suffering and despair.

Instead, focus on what you want to do, where you want to go, and what you want to be in the future. Making goals and plans for what you want to achieve will help you grow beyond your expectations. This mind-shift may appear unattainable. Success requires you to habitually focus on what you can do today to take small step towards tomorrow. So, go slowly and accept that you may slip from time to time. To make an amazing future, you need to put your energies into making that happen in the present. It won't come from your past, it is your now.

The future is unwritten, it's the choices you make and the actions you take that will decide what you achieve. To get yourself to a better place, you need to take full responsibility for your life and what comes next. Embrace your opportunity to shape your future. Embrace uncertainty. If you shy away from what may be, you will never know what you could have become. There is no reason for you not to pursue your dreams. No matter how old you are.

New York is 3 hours ahead of California, but that doesn't make California slow. Someone graduated at the age of 22, but waited 5 years before securing a good job. Someone became a CEO at 25, and died at 50. While another became a CEO at 50 and lived to 90 years.

—Anonymous

It's much better to try and fail than to never try at all. You will find joy in the journey, more so than in the accomplishment.

Stop Telling Yourself No

The biggest obstacle to achieving success is you. You can tell yourself, "All things are possible," or you can choose to say, "I'll never make it." The message you plant in your mind is up to you. Either way, you will be right. So why not choose to encourage yourself?

Too often, we discourage ourselves from achieving success with thoughts of "I'm not good enough", "I'm not smart enough", or "Why would they choose me?" These self-doubts will have you failing even before you get started. Instead of jumping straight into fault finding, ask yourself, "Why **not** me?" Releasing the past is about opening your mind to possibilities. No matter what happened before, you can achieve a new result going forward. Today is a new day and the choices are yours.

Considering all possibilities and taking advantage of every opportunity will lead you to the right ones.

Now Is All You Have

Focusing on now is the way to transform your future. By taking action now, you will move towards those experiences that will make a difference in your future. Everything you want, every accomplishment, every adventure originates with you taking action.

This book is part of that journey, inspiring you, revealing ways for you to consider new options, and providing hints of the next challenge you will encounter as you work to build a life for yourself that meets or exceeds your expectations. Choose to do the things that move you forward a little at a time. Day by day you will grow your life into one that you control and regardless of the surroundings.

We make tens of thousands of decisions every day. Those decisions move us farther down the road of life. They have the ability to transform us and take us nearer to the life we want to lead or limit us, moving us further from the life we envision. You cannot make those choices tomorrow or yesterday. They are in front of you today, at this very moment. Seize them. Win your day and step by step you will be victorious in your life too.

> *I think the biggest thing is just focusing on the day-to-day,*
> *your routine, not getting caught up in the future or the past,*
> *and just being right there and focusing on what you*
> *have to do that day or that night to help you win.*
>
> —Christian Yelich

Tying It All Together

Everything you've done, all your experiences, your successes, your failures have brought you to this point in your life. Now, you are looking into your future. Do you want to be swallowed up by those past experiences; the ones you keep hidden away, not wanting to share with anyone?

Or do you want to transcend everything that has come before, building on your life experiences to create and manifest more of the goodness that is inside you? The choice is yours. You can express your decision by taking a step into new uncharted territory. Don't look down. Focus on your ambitions and have faith that you were meant to chase those. That is what winning the day is all about. No regrets, courage in the face of fear, and a belief in yourself that you are destined to be an incredible person. Live your dream.

Here are some exercises to help you focus on living in the moment

- ▶ What is a past experience that has been extremely educational for you?

- ▶ What are some lessons from that you can, or do, apply to your life now?

- ▶ If you could do anything, what would you be doing a year from now?
  - ▷ Why?

- ▶ What are some tasks you can do towards reaching that vision?

- ▶ What is one thing you did today to make your life better than it was yesterday?

- ▶ What are some amazing things about you?

Get your free companion workbook for additional support at https://www.synergypersonaldevelopment.com/workbook/

5. Find a Purpose

As far as we can discern, the sole purpose of human existence is to kindle a light in the darkness of mere being.

—Carl Jung

For most of us, finding purpose makes life worth living. It creates wealth that can never be taken away. Living with purpose gives us a reason to get out of bed every morning and leaves us feeling content as we lay our heads down on our pillows each night. Yet, many of us find it difficult to focus in on what we are meant to contribute to the world in our lifetimes. Finding purpose can spark gratitude and connection, and you can discover yours by listening for your calling or creating yourself.

Listen to Your Environment

What were you born to do? Finding purpose from what comes naturally and in areas which you excel at puts you a step ahead.

You may feel the need to deny these skills and abilities because they make you stand out from your peers. Don't!

You were born to be special. Your natural talents are actually just a starting point. They give you opportunities to move beyond the norm and achieve unbelievable success if you are bold enough to embrace that. Many times in sports the best players not only have the most ability but also the strongest work ethic. They are the ones who show up early and stay late. These players work with private coaches during the off season to get just 1% better, knowing that those gains move them from great to all-stars and Hall of Fame level careers. If you are willing to put in the work, you can do that too.

What comes easy for you? There are things you do easily, and often dismissed as not a big deal, that are difficult for others to accomplish. Consider how you can use those abilities to make a difference in your life and the lives of others. Find steps to expand and develop these talents.

What do you like to do? Consider some things you like to do and how you can make an impact through those. Maybe you are like me, a generalist as opposed to a specialist. I dabble in many areas from music to neuroscience with just a sliver of knowledge in a variety of areas. This joy for education helps me to understand situations and people in novel ways that few others see. I can then transfer information I've taken from one source and apply it to another. Helping bridge gaps for others who have faced extreme difficulties or traumatic experiences in their lives.

While calamitous experiences create memories that you would rather forget, you have survived these deplorable experiences for a reason. As you are pondering why me? Consider what you can do to find a sense of purpose that takes you out of that and into an opportunity to help others who may find themselves in similar situations. Your horrific experience is not the end of your life, just a chapter of it. Now discover what comes next and unlock the powers to create change that have been growing inside of you, waiting for the opportunity to be utilized.

Such was the case with Louis Braille, who lost his sight at the age of three. Frustrated by the lack of written knowledge available to those that could not see, he invented the Braille writing system by the age of 15. Despite the system not being utilized in his lifetime, he continued to perfect it for uses in music, science and mathematics, textbooks, popular writing and correspondence. His system is still used around the world today as the de facto international written communication standard for the blind.

You may be like Louis Braille, finding the strength and purpose in your life through survival. Look those life altering experiences in the face. Then find the courage to make a difference in your life and the lives of others. If you are finding it difficult to surmount those experiences, take a deep breath and do what you can to put the past behind you. What's done is done, it's history. Focus on today, and how you can build yourself a brighter tomorrow.

If you have been fortunate enough to find talent and purpose through a serendipitous experience, such as a friend's suggestion to try a new activity, or perhaps you stumbled on a fresh idea that has meaning for you in a video, article, or class take the time to deeply explore these opportunities and the life changing effect success in one of these areas could have for you.

This is how I got started in writing. A friend suggested I try writing for an audience, and it has given me a way to share my ideas and experiences with more people than I could have ever imagined. It's possible that you are being guided towards a life changing contribution.

Above all, listen. Regardless of how it got there, a desire to contribute is sprouting inside of you, and it is up to you to discover and nurture that.

Create Your Own Purpose

If you have difficulty finding purpose in your life through listening to your environment and past experiences, you can manufacture it. Consider how you want to contribute and go for it. Take action every day or week, no matter how small. As you make progress, you will gain momentum. That force will help you through the slow times when you feel like your contributions are insignificant and a waste of time. They are neither. Sometimes the steps and success are visible and rewarding, and other times it's just a grind.

As you work to make contributions, take some time to get the bird's-eye view. Stop and reflect on your journey. That will help you understand the next few steps forward. Don't be afraid to readjust your methods and goals. With the clearer vision you have after you have gotten down the road a bit, you can chart more effective future steps.

The greatest achievement was at first and for a time a dream.
The oak sleeps in the acorn, the bird waits in the egg,
and in the highest vision of the soul a waking angel stirs.
Dreams are the seedlings of realities.

—James Allen

Still Not Sure? Look for Your Ikigai

Ikigai is a Japanese concept that means your reason for living. You can find your ikigai at the intersection of what you love, what you are good at, what the world needs and what you can make a living from. The confluence of these aspect of your life is where you will discover your purpose.

What you love and what you are good at is your passion. The things you love combined with what the world needs are your mission. What the world needs and what you can be paid for is your vocation. While what you are good at and what you can make money at is a profession. At the center of all these things is where you will find your ikigai.

My ikigai is transforming people into fuller versions of themselves. I love to support people and am good at educating people. The world needs more encouragement and positivity. My coaching and mentoring programs provide my clients and students the opportunity to grow as people, not just in the subject I am coaching them on, but as whole people. And finally, as I have developed my skills, I have been able to make a living as a mentor and a coach.

To find your ikigai, spend some time reflecting on each of the four key areas of ikigai (what you're good at, what you like, what the world needs and what you can make a living at). Then, spend some time pondering your passion, mission, vocation and profession, look for the similarities in these four areas, and how you can incorporate those into one meaningful and driven purpose. You do not need to complete this activity in a single day. In fact, you may find it beneficial to stretch discovering your ikigai out over a week or more. Concentrate on one area of the ikigai each day or over a couple of days, then consider the overlap areas of passion, mission, vocation and profession before coming to a conclusion on what your ikigai is and how to live it.

Tying It All Together

Reacquaint yourself with those experiences where you felt you had made a difference, even in the smallest of ways. Then focus on how you can continue to have an impact by taking action one step at a time. In addition, considering what you love, what your good at, what the world needs and how you can bring value in combining these areas will help you to discover your purpose.

Here are some exercises to help you discover how to turn your passions into a career or lifestyle

▸ What is something you've always wanted to try but haven't yet?

▸ If money were not an object, what would you do?

▸ What things come easy for you?

▸ What do you like to do?

▸ What can you be paid to do?

▸ Have you conquered a traumatic experience?
   ▷ How did you do that?

▸ What is a contribution you would like to make?
  ▷ What is a step you can take towards achieving that?

Get your free companion workbook for additional support at
https://www.synergypersonaldevelopment.com/workbook/

6. Your Life Is Your Responsibility

*You must take personal responsibility. You cannot change
the circumstances, the seasons, or the wind, but you
can change yourself. That is something you have charge of.*

—Jim Rohn

*I*t's easy to let someone else be in charge of your circumstances. You can choose to blame others for your misfortune or quickly reply with, "It's not my fault." When you take this route, you are surrendering control. Initially, it may be just one decision. Over time, however, it becomes a way of life, and soon you will be a prisoner in this web of surrender that you have sewn for yourself. It's time you changed that and seized responsibility for your life. This is the only way you will develop resilience as you clash with the challenges you encounter, working towards a life of meaning and purpose.

You Have Other Choices

Every situation you encounter provides you with options and choices. It goes without saying, those choices all have consequences. As you make these decisions, you will want to weigh the risks and rewards of each alternative.

One way to do this is to create a list of the ways you can take action, then devise a plan to change your situation. You could also brainstorm pros and cons for each option. Talking to others is another way to understand your situation and options. Another person's perspective may generate ideas you had not previously considered.

You can choose to accept your situation, saying, "Oh, well, there is nothing I can do about it."

Unfortunately, that won't get you very far. Accepting your undesirable circumstances will turn you into a constant complainer. That is a good way to get yourself a starting position on Team Blame. Team Blame's game is to throw every undesirable aspect of their lives to someone or something else, saying that it is outside of their control. "I did not get a raise because my manager doesn't like me." "I guess this relationship was not meant to last." "It's not my fault I was late, there was more traffic today than usual."

Accepting that the circumstances are outside of your influence is an easy way to cast aside responsibility. It may also temporarily make you feel better. In the long run though, you are blurring the lines of personal responsibility and tipping the scales of control and independence against yourself. Don't accept being a victim. There are many things you can change, be it with incremental steps or in one big shift.

The other option is to make a change. Don't just accept things at face value. Decide to make a difference. You actually have more control over your life than you think. It only takes one conversation to start a movement, provided you engage the right people. Confidently voice your concerns, describe the roadblocks, and seek solutions to those things you previously surrendered to.

If you did not get a raise, what could you have done to improve your job performance? Before your relationship falls apart, take a more active role in nurturing and developing it. Instead of blaming the traffic for your tardiness, leave earlier, find alternative routes or check the traffic reports to be more in charge of your morning commute. Don't accept mitigating circumstances. Plan and act in ways that establish your personal responsibility. Doing so will provide you more options and opportunities.

Setting Boundaries

If you find the situation disagreeable, you can remove yourself from it altogether. While this withdrawal may seem to be skirting the issue, it is sometimes better to cut your losses and move on. This type of realization takes some courage as you need to believe your talents, time and tenacity will be better served somewhere else. Removing yourself from a situation that drains your physical and emotional energy can light a fire in you to achieve more.

Be true to yourself above all else. Have a sense of what your efforts can impact and those situations which run counter to your ideals and beliefs. Commit your energy and presence to taking action that will make you a better version of yourself. Eliminate the circumstances from your life which fail to serve your development as a person of morals and integrity. You deserve that.

When considering exiting relationships, however, ask yourself where the problem lies. Is it with you? Is there something you can do to rectify the situation rather than severing it? It takes a lot of fortitude to admit our errors to others, but in admitting our faults and seeking forgiveness we not only strengthen ourselves but the relationship.

If the time has come to remove yourself from a constricting situation, it is important to be resolute and not give in to self-doubt. Separate yourself from the thoughts of remorse and regret. Those doubts will lead you right back to where you started. Wavering after you take such a big leap of faith can lead to dire consequences. You may find your position in a relationship weakened, or have lingering feelings of not being up to the challenge. Once you have decided to remove yourself, go all in to get out. Run, don't walk and whatever you do, don't look back. With some distance, your confidence will grow as you begin to realize you are now on a better path.

> *If you want to take responsibility for your life, you must choose to remove yourself from the situation, change it, or accept it totally, and you must choose now. Then accept the consequences.*
>
> *—Eckhart Tolle*

No matter which road you take, you will have setbacks—two steps forward and one step back. That's ok—it's still progress. We all make mistakes and then we work to get better next time. Don't be afraid of that. Failure sparks growth and growth leads to mastery. There is no way for you to become good at something without failing first. Believe in yourself, know you are destined to succeed and choose to be accountable for your progress through not only the failures but successes, too. No one else can do it.

As you take more and more responsibility for your decisions, actions and development, you will find new sources of energy. You will find the curiosity to be open to challenges. A new path will be illuminated that will present new possibilities many of which you may never have known existed. These doors which will open for you will be of your own making. Believe that you can be more, that you can do more, and that through this belief all things are possible. Have the courage to accept responsibility for all the aspects of your life that you have even the smallest influence over with uncompromising faith and belief in yourself. Afterall, it is your life.

> *The willingness to accept responsibility for one's own life is the source from which self-respect springs.*
>
> —*Joan Didion*

Tying It All Together

Humans tend to be lazy. We like to take the easy way out. We look for shortcuts and we would like to pass responsibility for problems around like we hand out business cards at a convention. You can choose to do that too. Or, you can stand up demand accountability from yourself, your friends and family, and thereby assert influence on your destiny. Refuse to accept that you have no control over your situation. Stop looking for problems and start looking for solutions. Regardless of where you are in life, choose to take some action now. Big or small, do something to take back control of your life. Then build on that. Only you can get yourself from the valley to the mountain top.

Here are some exercises to help you take responsibility for your life a step at a time

▶ What is an area in your life that you would like to have more control of?

▶ What is something you think you have no control over?
  ▷ How could you reduce the energy you give to that?

▶ What are 3 areas of your life which you could take more responsibility?
  ▷ What specifically could you do in those areas to make a difference?

▶ What are 3 areas that you need to set clearer boundaries in to protect your time, emotions, safety or the safety of people that matter to you?
  ▷ Specifically, what are those boundaries?

Get your free companion workbook for additional support at https://www.synergypersonaldevelopment.com/workbook/

Your Emotions

*O*ftentimes, our emotions overpower us. Strong emotional feelings can be paralyzing, leading to pain that makes us feel that we have no option but to continue on the same path. However, once you begin to understand that emotions are a type of communication from your nervous system to your conscious mind, you can take the next step of responding to those feelings, not just reacting to them. To better manage your emotions, you need to accept them, learn from them and then release those feelings, understanding that they have served their purpose.

In this part of Win the Day, you will discover how to read your emotions, interpret what they are trying to tell you and balance those signals with your actions, putting you more in control of your life. You will also get some clues into how to discover your passions and turn those passions into opportunities to grow and profit from what you truly love to do, regardless of your level of ability.

7. What Are Your Emotions Telling You

*Y*our emotions are a set of powerful tools. Abraham-Hicks, bestselling author of The Law of Attraction, calls them an emotional GPS. Experiencing emotions warns you of dangers, draws you into pleasant experiences and triggers an increasingly wide variety of responses that continues to grow as you understand your emotions and what they are communicating to you.

According to Joshua Freedman, the CEO and founder of Six Seconds Emotional Intelligence Network, there are approximately 3,000 words for describing emotions in the English language. If you do not have an adequate emotion vocabulary, you will naturally lump the description of your feelings into categories too small to effectively express what you are experiencing. One way to build your vocabulary of emotions is to use the Plutchik Wheel of Emotions, which you can find in the supplemental workbook.

Start by Defining & Identifying

Using the Plutchik Wheel of Emotions to identify emotions starts with understanding the eight base emotions: anger, anticipation, joy, trust, fear, surprise, sadness and disgust. Each of these has an opposite. Anticipation is the opposite of surprise. Joy is opposite sadness. Trust and disgust are opposites, and fear opposes anger. As you look at the wheel, emotions are identified across a scale. There are names for the different intensities of these feelings. For example, on the scale moving from sadness to joy we would experience pensiveness, sadness, grief, serenity, joy and ecstasy. You may have feelings of optimism and love in happier moments, while emotions like remorse and disapproval could be linked to those times you are feeling down. The wheel identifies 32 emotional states, using synonyms and antonyms that will bring your emotion vocabulary to well over 100 expressions, which is more than enough to start taking an emotional inventory.

As your build you range of words for describing emotions, take notice of your emotions and start to plot them on the wheel included in the workbook. Notice where those lie on the scale. What is the emotion's level of intensity? Does its fervor increase or subside over time? In less emotional moments, can you identify your feelings? Observing the levels of intensity as you plot your emotions on your emotion wheel will help you to identify them more easily when they arise and understand what they are communicating to you. This is a concept we will explore in the next chapter and in chapter 19 too.

According to Harvard neuroanatomist Dr. Jill Bolte Taylor, emotions that are not acted upon generally last only about 90 seconds. To enhance recognition of your emotions, you'll need to be able to identify them quickly. This will be easier as you increase your understanding of the words, or labels, used to describe them. The value in identifying emotions is not just in those 90 seconds when they are the most intense. It's what you do after that really counts. This will allow you to add fuel to or extinguish your emotions and reactions to them. Emotions have triggers. Considering what caused the emotion is almost as important as what you do once you have experienced that feeling. Intensifying or diluting the feeling is up to you. As your emotional intelligence improves, you will be able to consciously choose what happens next.

Emotions gave our pre-human ancestors two options: fight or flight. Today, however, there are many more options for responding to these signals. For example, we might need to consider a response, ask a question, or quickly invent a solution. By capturing the emotion, then pausing to consider how you will respond, you will begin to recognize emotions for what they are, a method for your subconscious mind to communicate with your conscious one.

The Catapult Effect

There are real dangers to just sweeping your emotions and the messages they are trying to communicate to you under the rug. A failure to recognize and effectively work through your emotions can lead to high levels of stress, anxiety and depression. Not to mention a wide range of physical and mental health problems. You can't fix a problem until you recognize it, and understanding your emotions is vital to your ability to diagnose problems, discover solutions and evoke pleasant experiences as well. The first step is always awareness.

It is important to realize that the discomfort that comes from your emotions is not a bad thing. It helps move you to another action. Emotions that you consider to be negative could be alerting you to a high level of risk or that you need to have more information about a situation before responding.

As scientists and emotional intelligence practitioners learn more about these sensations, it is becoming increasingly apparent that these feelings are a means of our nervous system communicating with our conscious minds. As a result, it makes more sense to read emotions as non-verbal messages and respond to them carefully instead of reacting immediately to the stimuli. Once you experience an emotion, stop and think about what to do with that information before acting. You will find that your responses are much more beneficial to your well-being when you add this cognitive step to your process.

In fact, you may find that the energy created by a bad feeling can be redirected in a positive direction. Transferring that emotional energy creates momentum that can move you towards your target at a force greater than complaining and anger ever will. I call this the Catapult Effect. The Catapult Effect states that if you first react negatively to an emotion, you need to get back to zero before you can move in a positive direction. However, by processing the emotion intellectually (at zero) and creating a viable solution without the emotional baggage, you can generate positive momentum that will catapult you forward towards your desired results with increased velocity. I call this the Catapult Effect.

So how does the Catapult Effect work? Consider Sue. It's late Thursday afternoon and Sue has just been given a big project by her boss that is due Monday afternoon. She could choose to get upset, or worse angry, about her boss dropping this assignment in her lap and spend most of the day Friday complaining about the assignment before finally accepting that it must be done.

Instead, she decides to take in the explanation of the project and its scope objectively. She asks questions that help her discover possible solutions, then returning to her cubicle goes to work on the initial steps to solve the problem. Within 60 minutes Sue has a plan for getting the project done on time without having to surrender her weekend.

She is now on target for competently completing the assignment. Conversely, spending a lot of time complaining to her family and coworkers is not going to solve the problem. The time she spent belaboring her situation could have been better used. The result of so much unproductive time is a completed assignment that is not as polished and professional as it could have been had she not wasted valuable time griping and grumbling. The difference in these results is the Catapult Effect: Positive, directed action in response to emotional stimulus yields better results in less time.

Tying It All Together

Emotions are neither good nor bad. They are a method of communication between your nervous system, your body and your conscious mind. By widening your emotional lexicon, you will more effectively identify your emotions, and be able to interpret with greater clarity the messages your nervous system is providing you. Then you can devise solutions that are intelligent and effective, advancing you in a direction that benefits your well-being. If this seems overwhelming, don't worry, we'll look more at how to use your emotions to your benefit in the next chapter.

Here are some exercises to help you become more aware of your emotions

▸ Using a Plutchick's Wheel, make a list of words for describing emotions.
  ▷ Create your own glossary of definitions for these words. You could make it a picture dictionary or create an intensity scale to nuance subtle differences.

▸ Keep a journal and identify emotions that you feel throughout the day for a week.

▸ What is a strong emotion you felt recently?
  ▷ What happened to trigger that?
  ▷ Did it increase in intensity or fade over time?
  ▷ How did you feel after it passed?

Get your free companion workbook for additional support at https://www.synergypersonaldevelopment.com/workbook/

8. Taking Control of Your Life

*T*om is a software engineer. Six-months ago, he got his dream job, working for a gaming company. He had a new girlfriend, a new, for him, BMW 3 series and life was looking great. Then, last week he got furloughed when work slowed down. His girl-friend found out a dark secret from his past that made her doubt her relationship with Tom. Being unemployed at the moment, he is worried about making the payments on his apartment and his car. Needless to say, he is uncertain about where to turn for sup-port or what to do next. His life is reeling, and it is all because of situations which are completely out of his control. Or are they?

There Is Nothing I Could Have Done Is a Myth

If you've ever felt like Tom and that life is stacked against you, it could be tempting to hold a pity party that last for days, weeks or even months. Instead, you will be better off if you get yourself ready for the next steps of your life. You can start by taking inventory of your skills, abilities and the things that are great about you. You saw how to do this in the previous section of this book. Using this understanding of yourself, build yourself into a person who is able to achieve their goals, whatever they are.

The world is not against you. In fact, the universe is conspiring for you. That's right, there is an invisible power that wants you to succeed. This comes from your belief in something higher, albeit a deity, the laws of nature, collective consciousness, or simply G.O.D—good orderly direction—belief in any of these concepts amounts to a belief in something higher than just yourself against the world. When you can focus on what is within your control and release what is not, you will find that a cornucopia of opportunities awaits you. Some you may foresee, while others you'll have no idea existed until they present themselves to you.\

Maybe Tom's work for a game developer was a sample of what is to come through the development of his craft. Maybe his new girlfriend wasn't meant to be in his life for long. Perhaps she served as a bridge to something better and a lesson for an area of Tom's life that needs attention. As Tom starts to focus more on solutions than problems, he will begin to grasp that his life is really on the upswing, despite the immediate and short-term signs suggesting otherwise.

One key for getting to a place in your life where things align in your benefit is to take action that moves your life forward. You can improve your skills, spend time with people who are important to you, and check things off your to-do list that keep you progressing. Focusing on what you can make happen instead of what happened to you will have you actively propelling your life forward instead of passively sliding backwards. Here are four things you can do today to take control of your life.

Stop Blaming Others

Your life is your responsibility. Despite how it may seem, no one has enough malice towards you (or energy) to spend time plotting your demise. If you think they are, why are you letting people like that into your life to begin with? Be stronger than they are by working on ways to improve yourself daily and choose to take more control of your environment. Most people are too busy with their own lives to actively spend much time trying to disrupt yours. Admittedly, there are people that feel a sense of joy when you fail—we will look at techniques for distancing yourself from them later when we discuss your environment.

For now, take the time to evaluate your situation and consider why quality opportunities are not coming into view. If employers are not calling you for job interviews, you probably need to make changes to your resume. If you are not attracting the right people into your life, it's time for an attitude adjustment. We often project onto others the traits and characteristics that we sense are true of ourselves.

For Tom, he could have been honest with his girlfriend about his past. This would have given him an indication of whether or not a relationship with her was worth continuing to invest in. He could have saved more money, to secure his finances in case of an emergency. He could even have done more research on the company before taking his new position to understand whether they would be able to retain his services long term. These are just a few of examples of the ways Tom could have taken more control of his situations and their outcomes. How can you take more control of yours?

Release the Things That Are Out of Your Control

Labels others place on you, the economy, or not getting an invitation to go out with people you thought were your friends are all things you have little control over. Dwelling on those will take you down the rabbit hole of anxiety and depression. Instead, work to understand what role you play in the things happening around you. Release those things you cannot control, and be more focused on improving the areas your efforts can impact. This will free your mind to focus on more constructive activities.

Apart from fixing my schedule for the future, I don't really think about what might happen tomorrow, the next day or a week later. Instead, my focus is on what I can do today. I want to make an impact and chip away at my goals. Need to strengthen a relationship? Try actively seeking that person out. Feeling that the j-o-b is unstable? Start watching senior managers for clues, prepare your resume and contact friends about potential job opportunities. Don't wait until it's too late. The earlier you take account of and responsibility for your situation, the more control you have.

Chose to Do One Thing That Moves You Forward

To be sure, this takes more than just flipping a switch; it is a complete change of mindset. There is a fine line between your influence on outcomes and control of decisions. You cannot control who gets promoted at your organization. However, you can influence the outcome by doing high quality work, offering to take on additional responsibilities and being professional. At the end of the day, if you are not promoted, take pride in your ability to provide high quality service for your company and those you serve. That is the measure of professionalism. Achieving the goals and milestones you set for yourself are victories that no one can take away from you.

You don't need a big action or grand result now to be successful. Take a small step towards your goals and the person you want to become. Capture that action on your calendar or in your journal. Over time your progress will materialize on those pages as clearly as the ideas in this story materialized out of my own reading and experiences. I note down what I have achieved during the day and how it has moved me closer to completing assignments, achieving my goals and overcoming obstacles. This journal has some valuable tips in it, since I am able to see the progress in black and white. I know where I stared, and the journal helps me to realize how I got to where I am now.

Life moves incrementally, not exponentially. Thus, the small steps you take today are the ones that will pay big dividends in the future. Life is a marathon, not a sprint. And this book is an example of moving forward in small steps. One chapter and one tip a day. After 30 days, you will have 30 tools for conquering stress, anxiety and depression As you review the ideas presented here, you will develop more techniques. Eventually, you will discover or create your own and soon you will have enough techniques and positive activities to make a visible shift in your mindset, engagement and confidence. As you are developing you will be able to count days that you won. Day by day, you will be victorious.

Look for Opportunities to Make a Difference in Your Own Life

If you are not looking, opportunities will never find you. Carefully evaluate your decisions throughout the day and make conscious choices about what you do. That is the basis of taking control of your life. When you consider how simple decisions such as what to put on your grocery list or what to do first thing in the morning shape your life, you will start making choices that are more meaningful and consistent with the person you want to be. These seemingly unimportant decisions will make a difference in your life over the long haul.

It is widely documented that we make an average of 35,000 decisions every day. Thirty-five thousand! Every time you say, "I don't care" or "It's up to you," you are forfeiting a decision. Start being more mindful of the decisions that have been placed in front of you. Consciously make choices as an exercise in seizing control of your life. Watch not only the outcomes, but also how your decision-making process changes. Over time, you will make better decisions and increase your confidence in doing so.

A caveat here is to be careful not to dismiss things you think are out of your control but that you do actually have influence over. For example, those friends who don't invite you out may not like that you become increasingly negative the more you drink, thus, cutting down on your alcohol consumption and resisting the urge to complain will make you a more desirable person to spend time with. When you understand that many people have a similar problem with you - then you are the problem. Take some time to work on improving in those areas. It takes a brave person to admit that they need to make some changes and actually do something about it.

Finally, don't create additional obstacles for yourself. Those recurring patterns and seemingly negative cycles you experience are a sign that you need to do something different to get past this life barrier. Look at your approach, your decisions, and your methods. Then decide if you're properly equipped to succeed. If you are not, ask yourself what you need to do to break through. The resources are undoubtedly at your disposal. You need to be open minded and consider your options. Then do something today to make the change you seek tomorrow.

Tying It All Together

At the end of the day, the control over your life solely rests with you. It comes in the decisions you choose to make, and the ones you forfeit to someone else. Be mindful of those and choose to be the determining factor in your life. There are events and circumstances that are outside of your ability to influence. Knowing the difference between the two will allow you to release the things that are beyond your direct control. This will alleviate your anxiety to some degree. Knowing the actions, you can take to move you towards your goals and make your daily life better is a vital step in being able to make progress. By the mile is a trial, by the yard it's hard, but by the inch it's a sinch. Do what you can to make a little progress every day.

Prayer for Serenity

This prayer may help you find the wisdom to understand that the only things you can control and change in life are your own attitudes and actions.

God, grant me the serenity
to accept the things I cannot change,
the courage to change the things I can,
and the wisdom to know the difference.
Living one day at a time,
enjoying one moment at a time;
accepting hardship as a pathway to peace;
taking, as Jesus did,
this sinful world as it is,
not as I would have it;
trusting that You will make all things right
if I surrender to Your will;
so that I may be reasonably happy in this life
and supremely happy with You forever in the next.

Amen.

Here are some exercises to help you find your path control of your life

► What are three things you can do to take more control of your situations (family, work, friends, environment)?

- ▶ Answer this question everyday: What is something positive that happened in your life today?

- ▶ What is something positive you are going to do tomorrow?

- ▶ How are you a more complete person this week than you were last week?

- ▶ Use a calendar as a journal and note your daily tasks, accomplishments and setbacks.
  - ▷ Then evaluate them at the end of the week and month.

- ▶ Note all the decisions you made today.
  - ▷ Mark with a plus the ones moved you forward?
  - ▷ Mark with a minus the ones you forfeited?
  - ▷ What were the causes of backsliding?
  - ▷ Would you take any of those decisions back?
  - ▷ How would a different choice in those impact your life?
  - ▷ How could you make a better decision next time?
  - ▷ What is a decision you can choose for an alternative course of action for tomorrow?

- ▶ What is an area where you feel blocked?
  - ▷ What would help you break through that?
  - ▷ How can you get that into your life?

Get your free companion workbook for additional support at https://www.synergypersonaldevelopment.com/workbook/

9. What Does It Mean to Be Truly Empathetic

*T*reating others with empathy is something we are taught from childhood. Our elders would often say, "put yourself in their shoes." Over time, we have come to believe that listening to and intellectualizing how others are feeling is enough. In reality, that is just the tip of the iceberg. Practicing real empathy is harder than that. It requires us to consider not only what but also why, others do what they do, feel what they feel and think what they think. When we can comprehend those with a little more clarity, we gain a deeper understanding of the other person, their needs and contributions while at the same time, increasing our understanding of ourselves. With this knowledge, we can enhance our thought processes creating deeper perceptions and more thoughtful responses.

Empathy is about finding echoes of another person in yourself.

—Mohsin Hamid

Understand Feelings

The first step of acting with empathy is understanding emotions. Our emotions are strong influencers in our decisions, both to attract and distance intended feelings. To get at the heart of another's emotions is to have a better understanding of your own as well. We looked at your emotions in chapter 7. And as you will see here, a core understanding of your emotions is crucial to your ability to recognize emotions in others.

When communicating with another person, consider initially how you would feel in their situation. Then ask questions to understand how they perceive the situation and why. Their view of the situation and needs may be different from your own, so listen deeply. This will help you understand what the person needs and how you can support them. You may want to start with a caveat, or introduction to your question, to set the context. For example: That is really different than how I would do it... I'm just trying to understand your thought process... or I'd never thought about it that way before... After that, you can ask more direct questions such as How do you feel about X? Why do you think that? What lead you to that solution? How can I help? When you understand the underlying cause of their emotions, and the other persons needs you will improve your ability to consider the issues from their point of view.

Empathy is about standing in someone else's shoes, feeling with his or her heart, seeing with his or her eyes. Not only is empathy hard to outsource and automate, but it makes the world a better place.

—Daniel H. Pink

Consider Preferences, Culture & Motivations

Beyond the feelings and emotions of others lie their cultural influences, personality and mitigating circumstances. Considering these areas takes a lot of patience. We often want to use our own lens to see the world. But thinking about the other person's cultural background (family, local, regional, and/or national), their experiences and their level of tolerance for novel and uncomfortable situations will help you to catch the nuances of what the true intention is beyond the words.

My friend Andy started a new job as a nurse's assistant. At his hospital many of the workers are refugees from Myanmar. They have difficulty learning Japanese and struggle to navigate the work environment. Some do not even like their jobs or living overseas. But with a civil war that has been going on since the 1940s and salaries in Japan more than seven times Myanmar's national average, these nurse's assistants seem like millionaires back home.

This puts a lot of pressure on them to stay in Japan and send money home to support their families. What's more is that they may even be considered celebrities in their hometowns and villages for the perceived success they have achieved. Even though inside they could be feeling miserable.

Andy could take some time to find out about what it is like to live in Myanmar, listen with interest and inquire about the challenges they are facing in this alien environment. Then ask how he can help. The insight he gets from these conversations will make him a better colleague and more empathetic to his colleagues' individual plights.

We All Act With Good Intentions

The vast majority of us want to see world peace, get along with our neighbors, and make gratifying contributions to our communities. When someone behaves in a way we judge as counter to this, we are quick to think they are undermining our or others good works. Instead of rushing to judgement, step back and consider how their action works towards achieving the results we are seeking (even as part of something bigger). Interpreting the solution from their point of view will help you work together to find more viable alternatives in unraveling bigger challenges.

Bob is planning on making a new recipe tonight, Chicken breast with roasted tomato. He needs those tomatoes to be soft and ripe. Unfortunately, all of them are a bit hard. So, he leaves the tomatoes on the counter in the morning before going to work with the intention of softening them up during the day. Mary sees those tomatoes on the counter and assumes Bob had forgotten to put them back in the fridge before going to work.

That evening when Bob returns home, knowing that he had left the tomatoes on the kitchen counter, he is sure he has lost his mind, confused by the fact that he could not find them anywhere. When he opens the fridge, there they are, just as fresh and hard as they were this morning. He gets angry and blames Mary for completely ruining his recipe before he even puts forth his best effort to make it.

When he asks Mary about the tomatoes, she says that she had noticed them on the counter and thought he had forgotten to put them away. Anticipating a tomato and cucumber salad as part of a nice summer dinner, and that these ones were in perfect condition for that. So she put them in a paper bag and set them back in the refrigerator.

Both people had good reason for their action and worked with the best of intentions for making use of those tomatoes. Yet without communication, their individual actions disrupted the plans of the other. Through an empathetic discussion, they will be able to decide whether to have the salad today or the chicken tomorrow.

We always consider the intentions of our own actions. However, when it comes to others, we focus only on the behavior. We usually don't take the time to consider their point of view, only considering the results as acceptable or unacceptable. Oftentimes, we incorrectly believe the other person's action was a deliberate attempt to stir up problems, create conflict, or foster ill will. That is just not true. Instead, we need to take the time to focus on the ideal that they had good intentions when deciding on and taking their course of action. After such consideration, we can work together to discover future steps that lead to mutually beneficial results.

> *The opposite of anger is not calmness, it's empathy.*
>
> —Mehmet Oz

Active Listening

Bob and Mary could have had a better understanding of each other and their intentions by using active listening to deeply comprehend each person's desires and intentions. Active listening has four stages: listen, paraphrase, ask digging questions and elicit solutions.

Using active listening, Bob would have asked Mary if she wanted the Chicken and Tomato dish tonight. If Mary had responded that it is going to be warm today and she would prefer something cool. The conversation may have gone something like this:

Bob: Mary, I was thinking of making that chicken and roasted tomato dish tonight.

Mary: I don't know Bob, today is going to be pretty warm.

Bob: (paraphrasing) Yes, it is going to be warm today. (digging question) Do you have another suggestion?

Mary: How about a tomato, cucumber and mozzarella salad?

Bob: (eliciting)That's a good side, how about the main course?

Mary: Since I am working from home today, I can roast the chicken this morning and then it won't be too hot tonight.

Bob: (confirming understanding) Tomato salad and roasted chicken, that sounds good. See you tonight, dear.

Mary: Have a good day at the office.

Problem solved; a little communication goes a long way. In this case, each person understands what the other wants and together they are able to come to an agreeable solution.

In our relationships, if we focus on how we can serve others and through our service inspire them to do the same, we can create positive momentum alongside a sense of understanding of those around us. Doing so enhances the quality of relationships by continuing to develop deeper connections and understanding.

3 Steps to Being More Empathetic

Be present

Focus your attention on the other person. Watch them as they speak. Listen for the words they choose, the tone in their voice and facial expressions. Really give them your undivided attention. Tune out everything else and focus on the conversation.

Pay attention to body language

Listen not just for what they say, but also how they say it. Look at their facial expressions. Notice if they fidget and their body positioning. These things are indicators of what is going on inside.

Test Your Understanding

Use paraphrasing techniques (I.e., so what you're saying is, do you mean, & let me confirm I understand you correctly) and draw conclusions based on the previous points. Then ask them if you are hearing them correctly. You can use this as a springboard for developing solutions together.

> *A prerequisite to empathy is simply paying attention to the person in pain.*
>
> —*Daniel Goleman*

Tying It All Together

Practicing empathy requires you to slow down, look others in the eye and consider situations from their point of view. You have to do more than put yourself in their shoes, you need to live in their skin for a moment. Asking questions and focusing on listening will make understanding the other person easier. While being truly empathetic can seem hard, practicing it at any level of ability will be appreciated by those you interact with. Like any skill, you can improve your level of empathy over time with effort.

Here are some exercises to help you develop your empathy muscle

- Consider a recent conflict or disagreement you have had.
  - ▷ What was the disagreement about?
  - ▷ What was your point of view?
  - ▷ What was the other person's point of view?
  - ▷ Why do you feel they had that opinion?
  - ▷ What questions could you have asked to have a clearer understanding of their idea?
  - ▷ What do you think their responses would have been?
  - ▷ After your analysis, do you still think they wanted what they were asking for or did they want something different (I.e., recognition for their idea, to get some help)?

- Practice active listening at least three times during the week. Use this pattern to become a deeper listener:
  - ▷ Listen deeply
  - ▷ Confirm your understanding of your counterpart's message
  - ▷ Ask eliciting questions to understand more deeply
  - ▷ Ask for permission to provide a solution, and if they say yes...
  - ▷ Respond to what you've heard with your own solution (omit this step if they don't want your opinion) Sometimes people just need to get the ideas out of their own heads.

- Ask questions like these to understand other people's situation better.
  - ▷ How do you feel about ...?
  - ▷ Why do you think that?
  - ▷ What led you to that solution?
  - ▷ How can I help?

Get your free companion workbook for additional support at https://www.synergypersonaldevelopment.com/workbook/

10. Four Words That Are Holding You Back

*L*anguage choices which create a defeatist view of your situation before you even start do you damage. They afflict not just your ability to succeed, but also your belief system, and motivation. In the first section of this book, You, we focused on how building a good relationship with yourself, avoiding negative self-talk and limiting language help you to feel more comfortable with yourself initially, and more confident as you continue to grow.

It is vital to be cautious of the language you use in self-talk. Once you choose words that limit your potential, it's a slippery slope. This often ends in unrealized accomplishments and failed dreams. However, removing confining words from your vocabulary will help you discover creative solutions for your problems and open the doors of opportunity to worlds beyond your consciousness.

Four Unproductive Words

But

But automatically discredits an idea. It indicates something is not true or possible for you. Using but limits your ability and fuels the belief that you are not good enough. Switching from *but* to *and* will enhance your creativity in finding solutions. For example, instead of saying "I would like to play the piano, *but* I have no musical ability," you could say "I would like to play the piano *and* if I give myself enough time, I will be able to play a few songs that I like." The impact of changing your language around this task will bring measurable accomplishment to your practice routine and playing of the piano.

Later

When you say *later,* you assume the opportunity will still be there whenever you take the time to consider it. Most people do not go back to consider those possibilities, as something else catches their attention. There are so many factors that need to align for anything to come to fruition that later pushes all those forces away from you. Once your momentum is halted, it is difficult to regenerate its energy. Later comes right before tomorrow, which is followed by never. If you need to put something off, schedule a time to take action, and give it your best. At least then, you are moving the opportunity into your sites.

Zig Ziglar used to ask, "Why is it that we never have time to do it right, but we always have time to do it later?"

Putting off until later or doing some tasks in a way that they need to be redone ends up taking up more of your time than it should have in the first place. When I was in 5th grade, I missed out on a chance to visit Alaska during spring break, because I put my homework off until the last minute. I thought the week off would give me time to do my best work. My brother, on the other hand, finished his homework early and was looking forward to enjoying his spring break free of school work. As a result, he got the opportunity to take an unannounced trip to Alaska with our father. How many unexpected opportunities have you missed because you choose to put things off or you didn't want to do them?

By putting things off until later, you risk never knowing what could have been possible. Don't get caught being too busy tomorrow taking care of things you should have done today. Instead, consider the opportunities presented to you as once in a lifetime chances and seize them immediately.

Can't

Can't is the killer of all innovation. It speaks to your own perception with little thought of the limitless possibilities just beyond your scope of knowledge. When you catch yourself saying "it *can't* be done," change your mindset to "How *can* it be done?" Only by accepting that a solution is possible will you be able to take the steps to achieve it. Thomas Edison said of failing to produce the lightbulb after thousands of tries, "I have not failed. I've just found 10,000 ways that won't work." Keep looking for solutions.

Try

Try by its very nature implies fail. When you take action, you are doing, not trying. Even if your attempt is unsuccessful, you can say I made an effort and I gave it a good shot. These expressions will help you, like Edison not only find some ways that don't work but also lead to the ones that do. Even, "I'll give it a shot," creates a better chance of success than "I'll try."

Limiting Beliefs

You deny yourself opportunity when you choose to say *try, but, later and can't*. They perpetuate untrue beliefs about yourself, others, and the world around you. Limiting language creates constricted thoughts. These bad words surrender control of your situation and opportunities to what others are willing to provide for you. It's better to take on life's challenges with a can-do attitude and keep in mind that all action is beneficial. It is beneficial because completing tasks moves you closer to where you want to be. Your thoughts provide the vision, your belief gives you the confidence to make an attempt, and your feats move you forward from where you are to where you want to be.

> *Thoughts are things, beliefs make them so,*
> *and actions solidify the beliefs.*
>
> —JB Glossinger

Give up your defeatist vocabulary, and focus on rephrasing your problems into challenges, your tries into efforts and your hesitations into analysis that will help you to work smarter, not just harder.

When you see an opportunity, grab it. Don't worry if the timing is not right or that you're not ready for it. The perfect time for you to act is now. That is why you are seeing the steps leading to that possibility in front of you. While in motion, keep that momentum moving forward, get something else done and knock another item off the to-do list. This frees you up for the unexpected.

Change Your Words, Change Your Thoughts

These four techniques will help you to move in a more positive direction and reduce the impact of limiting beliefs on your life. Remember, it all starts with a belief in yourself.

> *Where focus goes energy flows*
>
> —*T. Robbins*

Reframe

Change the words you use to describe your thoughts. Practice changing your statements from negative to positive. You can start by using *and* instead of *but*, replacing *can't* with *how can* and *later* with *now*. Then take decisive action on those thoughts until they become ingrained habits you do with little thought.

Take note of the language you use when faced with a challenge. Write it down and later review how you can make your statements more positive. For example, I'll try to meet your deadline could become I'll do my best to meet your deadline. In these examples, the idea is the same but the inference is completely different.

Other positive framings are problems becoming challenges and failures viewed as learning experiences.

Take action

Don't look for excuses not to do something which could be a turning point in your life. Take action today. Excuses and reasons are forms of procrastination that hold you back from your real potential. You will never know what you are capable of until you act, fail, and act again.

Initially, it's not the result that is important but the action. As you make bigger strides, you can set the bar higher and expect more. Initially, however, just focus on taking action. Completing projects task by task, redoing things that can be better and moving forward gradually will pay big dividends if you consistently take action.

Reflect

What is creating your roadblocks? How can you take your skills, abilities and goals to a higher level? Set some time aside to be alone. Reflect on and analyze where you have been. Then consider what you need to do to take the next steps towards where you are going.

One thing that I have learned in writing this book is that always being busy does not provide the opportunity to get better. This is true because we also need some time to analyze our efforts, progress and missteps. That analysis is where the real growth happens. As you are reflecting, remember to keep your dialogue positive and consider that you are taking steps forward regardless of the outcome of your actions.

Positive affirmation

Use positive affirmations to focus on achievement and strength, not weaknesses and problems. Say *I can, I will and I am* to increase your confidence and build a belief that you are capable of achieving whatever you set your mind to. As Brian Tracy, motivational speaker and author of more than 80 books, says, "What you think about, you bring about." Create your own short and vivid affirmations to steer you through troubling times.

Tying It All Together

Avoiding negative self-talk; instead using positive inner-dialogues will help you to remove doubt from your life and welcome possibilities of achievement. Too often we focus on problems, and use limiting words leading us to give up before we even get started. Beyond *but, later* and *can't,* create your own list of limiting words and find suitable replacements that expand your possibilities to create positive outcomes. Those will open your mind to solutions and discovery of endless possibilities. It all starts with the way you perceive yourself and your situation. Take what you have and do your best with it.

Here are three exercises to help you have more positive inner dialogues

Reframe –
- ▸ Write down some limiting self-talk or language you used.
  - ▷ Reframe it positively.
    Here are two examples:
    That customer is always causing problems –
    Reframe: *That customer challenges me to provide a higher level of service.*
    She is always complaining –
    Reframe: *She has high standards.*

Take Action –
- ▸ What is something you were concerned about and took action on?
  - ▷ What were the results?
  - ▷ What are the next steps?

Reflect -
- ▸ What is something you learned from a task you worked on?
  - ▷ How could you do it better next time?
  - ▷ How has that challenge helped you to progress?

Get your free companion workbook for additional support at https://www.synergypersonaldevelopment.com/workbook/

11. Get a Daily Dose of Positivity

*Y*our mind needs its daily helping of nutrition, just like your body. What kind of nutrition does it need? It needs positivity for you to feel good about who you are and what you're doing. You know what they say, "You are what you eat."

Too often we sit down and read, or watch the news, which mostly focuses on the negative without providing solutions for how things could be changed. This constant diet of negativity shapes our perspectives. To be more positive, you need to shift your time away from these negativity snacks and towards a healthy diet of positivity and prosperity. More conscious choices of the media you consume and the way you spend your time will help you to move your thinking toward an increasingly positive way of thinking.

Introduce Some Positive Ideas

As I mentioned in the last chapter, filling your mind with positives will help you to reduce doubt and the feeling of helplessness.

Getting positivity is not something you can do just one time and expect lasting results, you've got to take your positivity daily. The world's most successful people know this and they pay top dollar just to be in the presence of eternally optimistic people. You can do that too, inexpensively through video channels, podcasts, books and websites.

Whether you choose old masters like Zig Ziglar, Earl Nightingale and Wayne Dyer, or a newer breed of motivational experts like Nick Vujicic, Richard Branson and Seth Godin, you will find that starting your day with a spoonful of their positivity will help you to feel more confident and in control throughout your day.

Positivity also helps you to keep limiting beliefs at bay. Limiting beliefs like "I can't do it", "I deserve to be unhappy." "This always happens, so why should I expect anything different?" create a deep pain inside that traps you in your situation

Louise Hay said, "If you accept a limiting belief then it will become a truth for you."

This reality is that you will become what you expect of yourself. The corollary to her quote is if you accept that you can succeed then it will become a truth for you. In other words, you have the ability to carve out the life you want, so long as you are committed to achieving it.

Actions like working out, learning a musical instrument or taking a new job all have growing pains and learning curves associated with them. If you were to give up too early, you would never realize your full potential. So, the measuring stick needs to be what you expect to experience and how you define success. Then you will have a clearer understanding of if you are you moving nearer to or further from your vision. If you're getting closer, don't give up.

Manufacture Positivity

Another way to infuse your day with positivity is through affirmations. Positive affirmations are self-talk that focuses on what you can do and what is positive in your life. Doing affirmations helps you to increase your optimism and feeling of achievement. These help to chase away limiting beliefs that hold you in patterns which restrict your confidence in yourself and what is possible in your life.

Here are 10 examples of positive affirmations. Use these, seek out others specific to your situation or make up your own.

1. Day by day in little ways, I am getting stronger.
2. If my mind can perceive it, my will can achieve it.
3. I will be the best version of myself today.
4. The only thing that stands between me and success is me.
5. This day is blessed, it is up to me to use its precious gifts.
6. I am a winner.
7. By meeting life's challenges today, I will be more prosperous.
8. I will defeat my demons today.
9. The challenges I face today will make me a better person tomorrow.
10. At the end of the day, I will find pride in something I accomplished today.

Spiritual readings are also beneficial. Create a habit to take in a few verses or pages a day. This will give you a broader perspective on the issues and conflicts you face throughout the day, opening your mind to a plethora of opportunities you may not have considered otherwise. Enjoy these readings by ingesting them slowly, word by word. Let the ideas and concepts that resonate with you stick in your long-term memory so that you can recall their lessons in the future.

It is much better to read these texts yourself instead of reading someone else's interpretation of them, because the reading will uniquely speak to your experiences, beliefs and values. This will allow the passages to have a deeper impact on you.

Share Your Joy

Once you have let positivity in, it is hard to close the door to it. Eventually, you will start experiencing a more optimistic outlook on life. In order to continue the momentum, you need to share your newfound enthusiasm. Spreading that good feeling will not only enhance your life but the lives of those around you as well. Being observant of the change, you will find that your moods are contagious. So deliberately sharing positivity will help you to change your thought patterns and invite opportunity.

In addition, increasing positive self-talk reduces the space for negative ideas. Self-talk, your ideas and internal dialogues, has a large impact on how you interact with the world around you.

Tying It All Together

Finding ways to entertain positivity in your daily life will help you to have a more optimistic and happy disposition. It will aid you when you are facing challenges as well. A dose of serendipity will lead you to more creative ideas and make you more pleasant company for others as well. Still, it does take reinforcement to keep moving in the right direction. What you focus on expands, so choose to focus on the positive aspects of your situations and accept the challenges as ones that are moving you closer to what you want to achieve.

According to the Mayo Clinic there are several benefits to being positive, those include: increased life span, lower rates of depression, better psychological and physical well-being, better cardiovascular health and reduced risk of death from cardio-vascular disease, and better coping skills during hardships and times of stress. So, why not consciously welcome positivity into your life?

Here are some exercises to get your positivity circulating

▶ What are three sources of positivity you can access every day? (3 lines)

▶ Start by using any of these ten affirmations at three criti-cal times of day:
  ▷ First-thing in the morning,
  ▷ When you feel under-confident
  ▷ Before bed.
    1. Day by day in little ways, I am getting stronger.
    2. If my mind can perceive it, my will can achieve it.
    3. I will be the best version of myself today.
    4. The only thing that stands between me and success is me.
    5. This day is blessed; it is up to me to use its precious gifts.

6. I am a winner.
7. By meeting life's challenges today, I will be more prosperous.
8. I will defeat my demons today.
9. The challenges I face today will make me a better person tomorrow.
10. At the end of the day, I will find pride in something I accomplished today

▸ Write five affirmations of your own

▸ In your calendar, or journal note when you do a positivity exercise
  ▷ Reward yourself after 5 days, 15 days, a month, six weeks, etc., for being consistent

Get your free companion workbook for additional support at https://www.synergypersonaldevelopment.com/workbook/

12. Finding Something to Love

I used to work in the video production industry. As a member of a small production house, I did everything: project management, writing, directing, editing, serving as production staff, and even doing sales. After moving to Japan to teach English, I wanted to find a way to continue using my video production skills. I took my camera and went out to shoot nature. I edited those clips into mindfulness videos and created a podcast. Then I went on to produce it for almost five years. At its high point, Relaxation Media was the #1 wellness video-podcast worldwide on iTunes and had nearly 10,000 downloads per episode.

The ancillary skills I learned to support the podcast: creating a website and updating it using a content management system (CMS), writing a blog, and marketing allowed me to do a career switch a few years later, becoming a brand manager for a company in the entertainment industry and marketing some of the biggest pay-per-view events ever including Floyd Mayweather vs. Manny Pacquiao and Canelo Alvarez vs Floyd Mayweather. My efforts contributed to the company I worked for earning tens of millions of dollars, and I didn't do too badly either. What skill do you have or want to learn that can help you to contribute more to your work, community, or the world than you do now?

Become the Expert in Your Network

To create an upward spiral for your life, it helps to have an appreciation of something beyond the day-to-day grind. It can be a personal or professional interest. The key is to enjoy it. Having passion for something allows you to experience struggle without stress, learning without fear of failure and a whole new perspective that carries over into other aspects of life, too.

A deep dive into developing your abilities will allow you an outlet for your underutilized skills and talents. Continuing to develop those aptitudes will provide you opportunities to stretch your knowledge and try things on the cusp of your abilities. This is a great way to grow.

It used to be that you would go to university or learn a trade, then hunker down in a profession for years at a time. After work and on weekends you were free to enjoy your time off, and you could do whatever you wanted. When Monday rolled in, it was back to the grind. Today's working environment is quite different. People are finding ways to turn their interests into side hustles and new occupations. Regardless of your interest, from gamers and coders to spiritualists and artists, there are so many ways to profit from what you love to do, financially or otherwise. That pursuit of your interest and developing specific abilities is easier than ever before.

Here is an additional professional example from my own life that you can apply to yours as well:

I was introduced to emotional intelligence, EQ, through a unit I taught in an advanced English class a few years ago. This really interested me. As a result, I read books, watched videos, and created a learning plan to continue improving my own emotional intelligence. These activities helped me to gain a depth of knowledge, first about how to describe emotions, then how to analyze the message they are communicating, how to show empathy and interact with others in a way that serves them better. Initially, I was able to pass on my emotional intelligence literacy to my students. And now, it is a key foundation of this book and a pillar of my coaching practice.

Discover

Try those things that pique your interest, even if they seem outside of your realm of usefulness. Those whispers are unlocking doors to a more expansive version of yourself. Immerse yourself in the activity for a time. It may be a few days or a couple of weeks. You could do this by reading some books or articles, watching online videos, or even taking a course or some lessons. Take the time to sample a topic, become familiar with it and apply some of your learning. This will help you to understand if the subject is something worthy of deeper exploration. You may find that superficial knowledge is sufficient for you today, and that is ok, too. You may also find that by broadening your depth of knowledge you are able to change your future.

If this is something that lights a fire within you, create a learning plan. You could take a course, join a group, or continue a deeper dive into books, articles, and videos. Whatever you decide to do, commit to it for three to six months. That will give you time to raise your knowledge base past a level of curiosity and achieve a deeper appreciation of the area. In three to six-month's time you will firmly know if this is something you want to continue to pursue.

I see this in my study of guitar. There are people who have studied for years and made only modest progress, learning a handful of songs. Still, they enjoy playing. Others see a deeper world of music theory, improvisation, or an endless journey of discovery, so they continue to play. At whatever level, your interest is piqued. The activity will help you to become a fuller version of yourself.

Apply What You Have Learned

Now that you have a more rounded level of knowledge, you could continue to learn by teaching. Your knowledge is on display when you apply what you know to help another. This solidifies the information in your own mind, too.

When you teach, you need to be able to explain the ideas and concepts in ways that others can understand. This challenges you to think about the topic from all angles. If there is a gap in your knowledge, you will know it. That will help you to continue your development. Likewise, if you can present the information in a useful way, it will be clear to you that you have a firm grasp of the foundations of that subject.

As you find activities that you can mentally engage in, that interest will help you to expand your mind, resulting in increased mental capacity and creativity for handling all sorts of other situations. As your toolset grows, you will also more creatively solve problems and handle conflict. As a result, you should feel less stress and anxiety when you have to cope with dilemmas.

Knowledge is power. Applying your untapped and newfound abilities across vastly different situations helps to raise your overall confidence. Whether your new talent is a hobby, a professional interest, or a completely new endeavor, study what you love and become skilled enough to apply what you have learned skillfully.

Growing your skills in an area where you have interest also creates freedom to explore and the ability to become an expert. Doing this will also give you an activity that you can do as a positive release when you feel stress or anxiety. It's also better than sitting in front of the TV or computer for hours on end. Finally, developing your abilities is an investment in your future. As you learn and apply that knowledge, you are making yourself more valuable in every situation.

An End to Imposter Syndrome

We have all felt that we were imposters at one time or another, whether we were being paid too much, given an assignment we considered to be above our ability or teaching someone to do something we are underqualified for ourselves. The best remedy for these is to continue building your skills. Developing skills and applying those increases your personal credibility. As you build confidence in yourself, you will unreservedly not feel like an imposter anymore.

Tying It All Together

Growing your skills and appreciation in areas outside of those required in your daily or professional life will expand your consciousness. The development of this knowledge and/or skill will allow you to learn without stress because you find joy in the process.

As you continue to develop your ability, use it to educate someone else. This will test your understanding and raise your confidence. As you share your newfound talents with others, you will validate your knowledge. This will also help to eliminate feelings of being an imposter and replace those feelings with the awareness that you are an expert in your circle. Such confidence will carry over to other aspects of your life too.

Here are some exercises to help you discover or expand on a passion

▶ What is a skill or ability you have that you are underutilizing?

▶ How could you use an untapped skill or ability to provide value to someone else?

▶ What are three things you have always wanted to do, but never tried?
  ▷ How could you give yourself an introduction to one of those?

Get your free companion workbook for additional support at https://www.synergypersonaldevelopment.com/workbook/

Your Environment

*I*n this section of Win the Day you will discover how to have more control of your environment, from the people you choose to associate with to the processes you use to move your life in a more positive direction. At the end of the day, you are the master of your life—you control the decisions that will propel you forward or keep you stuck where you are. Hopefully, your choice to read this book inspires you to take action, choose to move forward and live, not merely exist.

This section is probably the most bold and frightening of the book, because it will challenge you to think in a new way, do things that you may not have considered before, and have you feeling uncomfortable as you contemplate taking on these new challenges. To unlock the power you have inside and overcome the past you will need to take more responsibility for yourself and your environment. Stop comparing yourself to others and create systems that allow you to feel successful more often. Life is a series of tests and this section will give you some powerful tools to surmount the obstacles you face and succeed on a daily basis.

13. Choose Your Friends Carefully

*M*ore than any other aspect of the outside world, your family, friends and associates play a big part in how you perceive yourself. Some cheer when you succeed, making you feel great. Others get jealous and try to find fault with your accomplishments, leaving you to feel embarrassed or ashamed of doing better than they have. In order to tip the scales of positivity in your favor, carefully examine all the relationships you have, including those with family members. You may have heard that, "Blood is thicker than water." This is, however, incorrect. The full quote is "blood of the covenant is thicker than water of the womb." Thus, those who you have alignment with, your tribe, are the ones who will see you through. That being said, make more mindful decisions about who you share your story and time with.

Drainers, Maintainers & Propellers

There are three types of people you will find in your relationships. Knowing which you are will help you to become a better friend. Identifying the types of people around you will help you to manage your environment more effectively. One of my mentors, Mike Lee Kaneric, who is a commando veteran of the Israeli Special Forces and member of the Black Belt Hall of Fame, identifies these three types of people as drainers, maintainers and propellers.

Drainers are those people who make you feel bad when you succeed. They appear to want you to have victories, but only as long as there is some benefit for them. They may throw up obstacles like, "that's too difficult" or "there are 10 people applying for that job, you'll never get it."

They could secretly be plotting your demise by flirting with your partner or complaining about your performance to a colleague or worse, throwing you under the bus to management. If you have drainers in your life, be very careful about your relationships with them. You may think you can find some benefit in these relationships, but you will spend a lot of time putting out fires and working on damage control to maintain these relationships. You may also find yourself on a slippery slope of becoming a constant complainer, just like these toxic people. Ultimately, you'll need to confront whether or not it is worth maintaining these relationships and prune them if necessary. Yes, it may be in your best interest to cut these people out of your life if you want to become more of what you like about yourself, even if these people are your parents or siblings.

Sure, I have friends, plenty of friends, and they all come around wantin' to borrow money. I've always been generous with my friends and family, with money, but selfish with the important stuff like love.

—*Richard Pryor*

Maintainers want you to succeed, so long as you don't do better than they do. They like you just the way you are. They will feel threatened as you grow, thinking that you will have no more space in your life for them. These are the people who are good for you as long as things are going well. When you are facing hardship, however, they will all but disappear.

Maintainers may be hesitant to tell you the truth when you ask for their opinion because they don't want to hurt your feelings or cause conflict. That is well intentioned enough, but it does not help you to grow as a person or get you closer to your goals. It could even lead to potential problems when their feedback is, "this presentation is good," but later you realize there are gaping holes in it that lead to a poor performance, or worse, a loss of credibility with your audience.

> *False friendship, like the ivy, decays and ruins*
> *the walls it embraces; but true friendship gives new life*
> *and animation to the object it supports.*
>
> *—Richard Burton*

Propellers are the people that help you to advance in your life regardless of the situation. Not only will they be there during your successes, cheering louder than anyone, they will also offer genuine support when things don't go well. Propellers believe in you 100%. That is why they will point out your blind spots and give you fair and honest feedback.

It may seem like your propeller friend is always nagging you, but that's because they see the potential that is inside of you and they believe in you. As their name suggests, propellers are often inspirational, helping you to get further than you could on your own. These friends sometimes demand more of you than you do of yourself, holding you accountable to what they believe you are capable of achieving. You may not always see eye to eye with your propeller friends, but unlike drainers and maintainers, they will never stop believing in you. While you might be comfortable where you are, they will encourage you and support you to move outside of your comfort zone to achieve your dreams. If you have propellers in your life, hold on to them. They are the people that make life beautiful.

My inner strength comes from my friends. I have a very close group of friends and family, and we all help each other through our dark times.

—Kathy Bates

Now that you know the three types of relationships, what kind of friend are you? If you are a drainer or a maintainer, what are you worried about? Surely, you would improve your own life by being a part of your friends' success. Find ways to offer opportunities and demonstrate your belief in them. This is quite a gift to give the people you care about.

Real friends know that we get more by giving than we ever receive by taking. Sure, there are trade-offs in relationships. These exchanges need to go back and forth to keep the friendship healthy and continue strengthening its bonds. That's reciprocity, focusing not just on your benefits but also on what you can give to others. These propeller relationships grow both of you. As your friends become better you do too.

> *Love is patient, love is kind. It does not envy;*
> *it does not boast; it is not proud. It does not dishonor others;*
> *it is not self-seeking; it is not easily angered, it keeps no*
> *record of wrongs. Love does not delight in evil but*
> *rejoices with the truth. It always protects, always trusts,*
> *always hopes, always perseveres. Love never fails.*
>
> *—1 Corinthians 13:4-8*

Defining Who Is Who

Make a list of your friends, close colleagues and the family members you spend the most time with. Then put them into these three buckets: propellers, maintainers, and drainers. Once you have done this, consider ways you can strengthen your relationships with the propellers. Likewise, begin separating yourself from the drainers, leaving them behind. Are there people you admire and would like to add to your friends list? Why not reach out to them? The worst that could happen is they don't reply to your request, and you are exactly where you are today. One way to kindle a relationship with new friends is to do something for them. This demonstrates that you have their interest in mind and are not just focused on your own desires.

Personally, I consider how I feel and act when I am around different people. This helps define the drainers, maintainers and propellers in my life. I choose to spend time with those who make me feel like the person I want to be, the best version of myself. I limit my time with the people who bring out the worst in me. This change has allowed me to reach higher heights and made life feel less like a rollercoaster ride.

Life Brings the Relationships You Need

As we travel through life, we meet many people some enter our lives and vanish just as quickly, while others we encounter will continue on with us for a long time. Regardless of how long or short, these relationships play an important role in our mental, spiritual and emotional development.

The first type of relationship is a bridge. Bridges help you to get you from one place in life to another. Teachers are a good example of bridges. They come into your life for a relatively short period of time and provide knowledge or experiences that you will use to make progress in your life.

Opposite to bridges are detours. These are the people that distract or take you off course from your intended path. Often when you resist change or want to avoid life's challenges detours will enter your life. Think of friends that divert you from the things you know you should do. If you are in a relationship with a detour, they may be providing you a rest or giving you a point of view different from your own. It is likely these relationships will end as quickly as they began.

While bridges and detours influence your life for a short amount of time, ferries will go along on the ride. Sharing your experiences and growing with you for a longer period of time before you disembark. There are both long ferry rides and short ones. Many deep friendships and long-term relationships are ferries. These relationships will be critical to your development while you are in them, but eventually you will need to exit the ferry because you've grown as much as you can from the voyage and you end up outgrowing the relationships over time. Sometimes you will reacquaint with ferries, since you have grown individually and can help each other to make additional progress years after you last met.

Not all relationships are transitional, but most of the people we meet in life are not meant to travel with us forever. Consider why the people in your life are there and how you are intended to develop from the connection.

Tying It All Together

When I meet new people, first I consider how I can help them. While this may overwhelm some, I consider it akin to offering a hand in friendship. As I engage with these people over time, I make an effort to consider their present needs and the benefits for both of us in continuing the relationship, then reinvest in growing those that appear to be mutually beneficial.

As relationships develop, I categorize my friends and acquaintances into the propeller, maintainer, or drainer bucket, and interact with them accordingly. This may upset some people, but it will not dismay those that understand the value of real friendships. For your part, be a propeller to the people in your life, cheer for all their successes and support them when they fail. By giving honest and helpful feedback, advice and support, you will show that you believe in them. When there is an opportunity to help a friend or acquaintance in need, take it. Then look for people who do the same for you.

Reflecting on the relationships you have had in your life and the ways you have developed through them will help you to consider the types of relationships you need in your life now, and in the future. These new relationships that manifest themselves to you could be the ones that bridge gaps or transport you to a version of yourself you never imagined was possible without their support and insight.

Here are some exercises to help you have a better understanding of the people around you

- ► List 3 people you admire that you would like to have a better relationship with
  - ▷ How could you make a connection to them?
  - ▷ What is a friendship offering you could make?

- ► Write about a relationship from your past that has been influential.
  - ▷ Was this person a driver, passenger or bridge to something new?

- ► Consider why the people in your life are there and how you are intended to develop from the connection

- ► What kind of person do you need in your life to help you grow?
  - ▷ How would that kind of person help you (be as specific as possible)?

- ► Make a list of all your friends, colleagues and acquaintances. Then categorize them as Drainers, Maintainers or Propellers.

Get your free companion workbook for additional support at https://www.synergypersonaldevelopment.com/workbook/

14. Who Can You Turn to?

*T*here are so many important things going on in our lives that in order to understand their purpose we really need to share and discuss them. Whether those things are good or bad, it helps to talk about them with the propellers in your life. Who in your inner circle gives you their undivided attention, even if it's only for a few minutes? The dreams and difficulties you hold inside for fear that no one else could possibly understand you need to be shown the light of day. Rely on a trustworthy friend to test the waters of these situations, knowing that they will not pass judgement. When you talk about your joys and concerns you make them tangible, and getting them out in the open will give you a fresh perspective, allowing you to inspect and evaluate these issues in clear and vivid detail.

> *There is no possession more valuable*
> *than a good and faithful friend.*
>
> *—Socrates*

You may be thinking that you can't share your deepest thoughts with just anybody, and you're right. It is frightening to let those deep secrets out in the daylight. But there is no better way to face the issues that plague you and find viable solutions than to talk about them. Find a propeller and explain what how you want them to listen. For example, if you want them to be a listening post, you might say, "I'm so frustrated that I need to tell you what happened this morning." Or if you need advice, you might start the conversation with, "I am having a problem communicating with my daughter and need your advice." Start the conversation with your expectations for the discussion. That gives the other person context for how to listen and your expectations of their input. Be direct and tell your friend exactly what you want them to do. Real friends will respect whatever boundaries you set.

In order to find someone that you can share your deepest thoughts with you may be expected to hear what is burning inside them, too. Welcome the opportunity to build a bond and improve your communication skills. In actively listening to their issues, you may gain deeper insight into your own situation as well. Understand that if your confidant is a good listening partner but doesn't want to share their issues and challenges, you should also find someone else to help and pay forward their support. This allows their kindness to create a ripple.

Trouble shared is trouble halved.

—Dorothy L. Sayers

The best feedback is direct and actionable. If you ask for it, be ready to receive their comments. Good feedback tells you something you can do right now to move forward. Often action-able feedback is direct and harsh. You may wince because it is something you don't want to hear or have been avoiding, but take your medicine all at one time. You asked for the advice and you trusted the person you are talking with. Keep in mind that it is through compassion and good intentions (karma) that they are providing you advice. Don't take them, or their time, for grant-ed. Pay attention to and act upon your friend's advice to show that you really respect their input. You don't need to do what they suggest, but do take some kind of action. This goes a long way towards strengthening the relationship.

If you are unsure of how to take their advice onboard, ask more questions to understand the motivation and perspective they used to devise their solution. You may not fully agree, but consider the difference in perspective and how you could apply the advice. If you are not sold on their suggestions, create an alternative op-tion that moves you forward. It is vital that you take some action as a result of these conversations, otherwise it's just a pity party. Those don't serve anyone's interest.

Five Places You Can Take Your Problems & Concerns

Friends

Friends can be a great resource for talking through personal growth issues and persisting dilemmas. Real friends care about you and your progress. You have a shared history that may pro-vide a basis for deep understanding of your situation. Friends may be inclined to present ideas in a manner similar to the way you do because of the commonalities. For these reasons, they are a good resource for talking through your issues.

However, friends may not always listen deeply, or they may be dealing with their own overwhelming problems. They may still perceive of you as the kid from their childhood, or their drinking buddy whom they shared their woes with on Friday nights a few years ago. They may not see the version of you that exists today. That can be frustrating when trying to clear your current hurdle or get a fresh perspective on next steps to improving your life.

> *Trouble is part of your life - if you don't share it, you don't give the person who loves you a chance to love you enough.*
>
> —*Dinah Shore*

Mental Health Professionals

Psychiatrists, psychologists and counselors are all trained in the understanding of the human mind and how we handle crises. These people can help you cope with issues now based on conquering roadblocks from your past. They may show you new techniques for overcoming recurring problems or guide you through battles against your challenges one step at a time.

Coaches & Mentors

Professional-minded coaches and mentors differ from counselors and mental health experts in a fundamental way:

Coaches and mentors are concerned with your future progress, not your past.

As a professional coach and mentor, for example, my concern is where you are going, not where you have been. To me, you're the total sum of all your previous experiences, and you will carry that baggage with you wherever you go. This outlook is very different from what you will get when speaking with mental health professionals who often apply familiar labels to your situation in order to identify your predicament, or friends who may see things through their personal point of view.

Coaches and mentors are more mindful of your development. They will work with you on where you are going and don't pay much attention to where you've been, that is the realm of mental health professionals. Since their relationship with you is professional rather than personal, they are motivated to see you succeed. Unlike talking to friends, a coach's sole objective is your progress with no hidden agendas.

Mentors have often been through similar situations to your own. They acquired wisdom and share it through hindsight. This knowledge can help you avoid pitfalls and speed up your development, because you can learn from their mistakes. Working with a mentor can be a bridge that gets you past an obstacle or the relationship can be an ongoing one that guides you through your valleys and walks with you over the peaks too.

A coach, on the other hand, will help you improve specific abilities. You may seek a coach for public speaking and presentations, to manage conflict, or improve your relationships. Their advice will be more specific and directed towards solving the crisis of the moment. That is not to say they will not help you through other situations down the road. Some coaches will, while others are more specialized in particular issues.

Groups

Counseling, masterminds and other self-help groups are focused on bringing people together who are experiencing similar issues. They are good places to discuss your concerns with like-minded people. Because they have walked, or are walking a similar path, these folks will be more empathetic to you and the resources at your disposal as you manage this phase of life. In these groups you can fast track your progress because there will be people who have been where you are and can understand what you are going through. Some of them will have cleared those dilemmas others will be facing them just as you are.

These groups are often anonymous or confidential, so you can share your deepest thoughts without concern for who may find out about what you said later. Groups like AA are beneficial for keeping you moving down the path and handling struggles that can last a lifetime. While others, like masterminds, will help you to climb to the next peak. If working with a group sounds appealing to you, try it out and see if it is a good fit. If the first one is not, try another one. Good groups are about chemistry and they will all be a little different, even if the programs are the same.

Virtual Mentors

Virtual mentors are people who you learn from via books, websites, podcasts, etc. Some people like reading biographies and find insight from the lives of others. Listening to talks and reading books from motivational people like Randy Gage, Zig Ziglar or Dr. Wayne Dyer may also help you tap their experiences to find answers on your journey.

Virtual mentors have made hundreds if not thousands of hours of content available that you can utilize to develop yourself and find solutions to the dilemmas you face. While not communicating directly with these thought leaders, you are gaining a wider base of understating to apply in moving towards where you want to go. Digital mentors help you know that you are not alone and that others have walked a similar path to your own. Some of these mentors have communities or opportunities to share ideas through social media. Take advantage of those to connect to others.

If you choose to employ the do it yourself approach, you may want to write about your dilemmas and what you're learning through their insights to give voice and consideration to how those influential people would respond in your situation. Many a good solution has started with the words, "What would Nelson Mandela do?"

Tying It All Together

You need not carry life's burdens alone. There are people you can engage with that will provide you a fresh perspective on the predicaments you are facing. Consider what kind of help you need; an ear, advice, a new strategy or a model. Then seek out a friend, mental health professional, coach, group or even a virtual mentor. The clarity you find will have you wondering why you didn't do this before.

Here are some exercises to help you utilize the knowledge and experience of those around you

▶ What are 3 things you want to accomplish in the next 6 months?
  ▷ Who can help you to achieve those things?
  ▷ How could they help you?
  ▷ What advice would you want from them?
  ▷ How can you action that?
  ▷ When will you begin to take action on that advice?

▶ Make a list of your support circle
  ▷ How can each person help you with as you move towards a more complete version of yourself?

▶ Who are your trusted advisors?
  ▷ In what areas do they help you?

Get your free companion workbook for additional support at https://www.synergypersonaldevelopment.com/workbook/

15. Express Gratitude

*C*athy and Louise work on the same team. Cathy makes an effort to look good in front of the boss. Louise focuses on helping her colleagues. Cathy takes other's ideas and calls them her own. Louise looks for ways to get others to contribute to projects and gives colleagues credit publicly. Cathy says that one day she will be in an executive suite. Louise says we're all on the same team and is grateful for the job she has. In meetings, Cathy is short-tempered and talks a lot. Afterwards, she criticizes others for not being as bright as she is or for wasting her time. Louise is patient and encourages everyone to share their views, then thanks them for their input.

This year, the company had to lay-off several of its employees due to an economic downturn. Louise got a promotion. Cathy is looking for a new job.

Choosing to look at your life through a gratitude filter, like Louise does, will make every day richer, happier and more fulfilling. Be grateful for what you are experiencing, and how it is preparing you for your next big life event. Live with humility. Remember that your success grows not just out of your own efforts, but also those who have guided, supported and taught you.

As you give from your experience and expertise, you will not only be helping others but also developing your own abilities. This may seem like a big challenge, recognizing the contributions of others, but it will help you to broaden you vision of what is possible and enhance your sense of security. As we discussed in the last chapter, you are not alone on your island, there are others who support or are willing to support you, if you allow them into your life. Acknowledging their contributions takes some of the pressure off of you to go it alone.

Pride makes us artificial, and humility makes us real.

—*Thomas Merton*

As you begin to find success, it is easy to lose sight of the fact that your accomplishments were not achieved in a vacuum—the idea that your success is all your own doing is false. While you should feel proud of your development and accomplishments, also remember that you had help in navigating your trials and reaching the mountain top. One person recommended you for a position. Another taught you a vital skill. And don't forget about those who encouraged you when you were feeling down and defeated. All of these people and others invested their energies into you and helped you to find a better version of yourself. Whether you are working your way out of situations of anxiety and despair, or a confident person moving through your next challenge, the people who contribute to your achievements are beacons of hope. They light the way as you continue to grow.

Remembering these contributions will enhance your ability to be humble and motivate you to continue when it seems failure is inevitable, or your goals appear unachievable. Keep reaching, knowing that you stand on the shoulders of those who want you to succeed, and that their breaths fill your sails propelling you forward.

Humility does not mean groveling and living in a state of being unworthy. Instead, humility is the ability to share credit for success. Humility is knowing one always has more to learn. Having humility keeps you grounded, remembering where you came from and how your success was achieved. Even if your success is just making it through the day, a gracious thank you to those who supported you will enhance your ability to win tomorrow too.

One way to develop humility is to take an inventory of the contributions to your success. Make a list of people and situations that have helped you to overcome challenges and achieve success. Who had a hand in your achievements? What did they do? Once your list is complete, make an effort to appreciate those folks. You could write a letter, email or text; give them a call or video chat; or even say a prayer of thanks for them.

Another beneficial gratitude exercise is to make a list of things and people you are grateful to have, or have had, in your life. Then, review the list when you wake up in the morning this will help you to start your day on a positive note.

These things all create positive energy that transcends your own sense of accomplishment and help your gratitude to grow. I have found that expressing gratitude transforms selfishness to benevolence. It also abates feelings of contempt and jealousy. Outwardly expressing gratitude will help you to make more friends than you ever will being self-centered. When you live with gratitude and humility, you will experience an abundant life with limitless opportunities for everyone.

Just as others have helped support you through the darkness of your struggles and the challenges of your growth, pay it forward and carry the torch that lights the way for the next person. Slowing down and taking time to recognize when those around you need support and offering assistance will help you live a deeper, more meaningful life. This is also a way to build your empathy muscle. You can make a big difference in the life of another by the simplest act of kindness or support.

At times our own light goes out and is rekindled by a spark from another person. Each of us has cause to think with deep gratitude of those who have lighted the flame within us.

—Albert Schweitzer

Choosing to live with gratitude is a conscious decision and it takes work to flip that switch. Living with appreciation means waking up thankful every day: Grateful that you are able to live another day and take another step forward towards achieving the life you dream of. Be thankful for the opportunity to contribute in whatever way you are able to make your relationships deeper, your environment better and the world a more positive place. Feel gratified that, on this day, you can be the difference.

When you are living and acting with gratitude, you experience life as a divine gift that needs to be shared. You have a choice in how you face each day. You can start by finding what's wrong with the world, or you can focus on what makes it right. It's up to you.

We all start each day with a blank slate. Beginning with appreciation for some element of life and continuing to find reasons to be grateful as the day goes on results in a life filled with joy. Look for that joy and feel a sense victory in your accomplishments throughout your day. Look for opportunities to help. Then, take action. Don't focus on what you get today. Instead, concern yourself with how you are developing an abundant future. A future where there is enough for you and your neighbors too.

> *Often people ask how I manage to be happy despite having no arms and no legs. The quick answer is that I have a choice. I can be angry about not having limbs, or I can be thankful that I have a purpose. I chose gratitude.*
>
> —*Nick Vujicic*

Tying It All Together

Living with gratitude and humility makes life an eternal gift. More active recognition of that will transform your view of opportunity from something that is limited and out of your reach to something that is abundant and achievable, one step at a time. You will find that your life is manageable with the help of a support circle and a feeling that you are not in this fight alone. You are being supported by friends and strangers. As you grow, you can provide that support to others too. This way everyone wins.

Here are some exercises to help you grow your gratitude

▸ Make a list of the people who have had a positive influence on your life
  ▷ How have they done that?

▸ What are you glad to have in your life?

▸ What are 3 things for which you are grateful?

▸ What is something someone has done recently that you appreciated?

▸ Write 3 gratitude statements that begin with "I appreciate."

▸ Reflect on the blessings and contributions that you received today as part of your pre-sleep ritual

Get your free companion workbook for additional support at https://www.synergypersonaldevelopment.com/workbook/

16. It's Not What You Get That Matters

When I was a child Christmas was a time for making long lists of what we wanted and waiting to see what was under the tree. Back then, there was no greater thrill than having a mountain of presents to open and relish for the weeks and months to come. That all changed the year I discovered that the joy of Christmas isn't in what you get.

At the top of my cousin's list that Christmas was a stereo. Since I was just a teenager at the time, I did not have the money to buy her a new one. Still, I love music and knew how much having a way to play her favorite tunes would mean to her. I checked with her parents and found out that Santa wasn't going to be bringing the big gift at the top of her list that year.

Fortuitously, I was at a friend's house when he was about to throw out his old stereo, because the speakers didn't work anymore. Boom! I heard the knock of the opportunity elves at my door. I checked the turntable. It worked fine. So, I bought a new needle and rebuilt the speakers. All told, the project took me about a month and cost around $30. A modest price for such an excellent gift.

When Christmas came, I gave the stereo to my cousin. It's impossible to put into words how happy she was. I hadn't seen such overwhelming joy expressed by one person in my entire life. It was as if she'd won the lottery. Her happiness made me teary-eyed, too. When I thought about how my resourcefulness and skills had transformed something that would've ended up in the trash into a spectacular gift of immeasurable value, it was amazing! The delight that she felt was contagious. I would never have believed the outpouring of happiness I felt if I hadn't experienced it myself. On that Christmas day I learned a valuable life lesson: It isn't what you get that is important, it's what you give.

> *It is in giving that we receive.*
>
> *—Francis of Assisi*

Giving doesn't need to be limited to holidays and birthdays. We can give in so many ways and at any time. So long as you present your gift without the expectation of getting something in return, it has immeasurable value for not only the receiver but for yourself as well.

Merriam-Webster defines a gift as something voluntarily transferred by one person to another without compensation. Therefore, if you give with the expectation of reciprocation, that is a transaction. It is not a real gift. In order to appreciate the true value of your gift, present it unconditionally. Here are some ways to make giving a part of your life, and in turn create a greater sense of value inside of yourself as well.

No Reason

You don't need a reason to be kind to others whether they are friends or strangers. Little things that make others' days happier, safer or more fulfilled could have a profound impact. It just takes a little effort to do a random act of kindness. You could buy coffee for the person in line behind you, give a blanket to someone who is cold, or alert someone to a danger - avoiding something catastrophic. All it takes to provide some kindness is the desire to make the world a better place, and the willingness to act on that desire.

When things aren't going well for me, I often think about what I can do for others. This charity builds on my humility and gratitude. I feel a sense of accomplishment when I make a difference in the life of someone else. There is no better way to brighten a day than with an unexpected kindness, given or received.

> *I have found that among its other benefits,*
> *giving liberates the soul of the giver.*
>
> —*Maya Angelou*

Don't Give It a Second Thought

Whether you give money to charity, donate to your favorite podcast, internet radio station, or a Kickstarter campaign you can make a difference in the lives of others. This is also true of giving your time. For example, participating in a mentorship program, volunteering at your local soup kitchen or teaching English as a second language on your day off. Giving - no matter what it is- creates a situation where both the contributor and the recipient feel happier. Several medical studies have proven that giving stimulates the parts of the brain that make you feel happier, and we all want that.

When you make giving a habit, you're creating abundance in your life and the lives of others. You're sharing universal love and also clearing the way for more prosperity to enter your life. These acts of benevolence demonstrate what's possible with a little imagination and consideration for the world around you. Others will see your example, and some will seek to emulate it.

> *The human contribution is the essential ingredient. It is only in the giving of oneself to others that we truly live.*
>
> —*Ethel Percy Andrus*

What are you contributing to make the world a better place, in even the smallest way? The making of differences do not need to be large to be significant. You could document it as a way to remember and fill your spirit with joy every time you recall your acts of kindness. On a regular basis, consider what you have contributed to the world around you and then write it down. By realizing your contributions to society, you will enhance your sense of value to the world, and also to yourself. Increasing your sense of value will decrease your feelings of hopelessness and help you to grasp that you are making the world a better place. Only you can give from your unique perspective. We all would benefit from an outpouring of the gifts you have inside of you.

Documenting your giving helps you to recognize the kind-hearted person that you are and the value you give to those around you. Giving of yourself is the greatest gift you can give.

> *The more one forgets himself - by giving himself to a cause to serve or another person to love - the more human he is.*
>
> —*Viktor E. Frankl*

One thing that has become clearer as we have lived through the coronavirus pandemic and help each other is that we get much more by giving, than by taking. For example, ordering delivery meals helps local restaurants to stay in business. Giving larger than usual tips to service providers helps them to pay the bills that are mounting because there are less customers, and paychecks are lower. We can all make a positive difference in the lives of others if we just look for little ways to contribute.

When we focus only on what we can get, our perception of what's possible is very limited. If we see the world just in terms of what benefits us, then we give just enough to satisfy our sense of duty or personal gratification.

However, if we focus on the value we are infusing through our gifts, then the pocket we pull from is virtually botomless. This may seem unbelievable, but there are so many ways that we can give that positively impact the world. As a result, we will never run out of resources if we are creative in our giving solutions.

This abundant sense of contribution will provide the opportunity to make an impact regardless of your financial situation.

You can give your skills, your time, or items you no longer use or have need of. Gifts that come from your heart spread feelings of benevolence, good will and prosperity.

> *Let us not be satisfied with just giving money. Money is not enough, money can be got, but they need your hearts to love them. So, spread your love everywhere you go.*
>
> —Mother Teresa

Tying It All Together

Giving is the ultimate gift. When you give, you're doing more than making a contribution that aids others. You are enriching your own soul too. The act of gifting items, your time, service and/or money to help others allows you to make enriching contributions. Helping others on their journey to success or in finding moments of pure joy are the greatest gifts we can give.

Here are some exercises to help you become a better giver

▸ What is a gift (physical or otherwise) you gave for no reason?
  ▷ How did that benefit the recipient?
  ▷ How did you feel after giving?

- ▸ What is a random act of kindness you've done this week?
  - ▷ How did that make you feel?
  - ▷ How did it benefit the other person?

- ▸ What is a random act of kindness someone did for you?
  - ▷ How did that make you feel?
  - ▷ How did you, or could you, pay it forward?

- ▸ What are some simple random acts of kindness you could do?

- ▸ What are some ways you could increase your contributions to worthwhile causes?

- ▸ How have you made contributions in the past?
  - ▷ What was the impact?

- ▸ Write down some kindnesses given to you when you were having feelings of self-doubt or worthlessness.
  - ▷ How did those help you?

Get your free companion workbook for additional support at https://www.synergypersonaldevelopment.com/workbook/

17. Live One Day at a Time

Sam is a planner. She has great ideas about how to achieve more in her life. She created a 30-day exercise program to increase her stamina. She took several online courses to improve her professional skills. When she was having trouble in the relationship with her sister, she read a book about improving communication. Unfortunately, she never acts on these ideas because she is always waiting for the perfect situation to use them.

It's too cold to exercise today, so she gave up on that routine. She was assigned to a new project, so she failed to use the professional training. Even when the frost between her and her sister, Marie, melted, she forgot to try the communication techniques she read about as a means to strengthen that relationship. Sam needs to focus on consistently using the techniques that she is studying, there will never be a better time than now.

I am a firm believer that the reason we make plans or are introduced to new things, like courses and books, is that we are being prepared for new experiences. Missing the opportunity to capitalize on these insights is an opportunity lost. As we discussed before, later is just beyond our reach. Instead of finding reasons not to, make a choice to get started now.

The Past Is Gone

The past is a great place for reflecting on the many lessons you've already learned, and to consider how to apply those in the present. Realizing and learning about what you've done right and can utilize again will build your confidence. Lessons about what you could've done better will present you conquerable challenges that you will revisit in the future. Using reflection is a good way to learn from the past.

However, if you're living in the past, it will keep you from enjoying what's happening in your life right now. You'll always wish that things ended up differently from what they actually are. That regret can leave you feeling less than fully alive, it's as if some portion of your life is incomplete or missing. That won't help to bolster you feeling of self-respect or confidence.

The past is just that, the past. It's over and done with. You can't live there hoping things will return to the way they were before you made that mistake. Time moves forward. Those old memories will never be a part of your future. The reality is: Nothing will ever be the same as it was before. To live in the past is to deny yourself the opportunity to grow into the person you were meant to be.

While your previous experiences may shape the person who got out of bed this morning, they don't define who you are today or who you will be tomorrow, unless you let them. Every day provides the chance to reinvent yourself. Learn life's lessons, enjoy the memories of those by gone days, and work to make new ones.

> *The past is a great place and I don't want to erase it or to regret it, but I don't want to be its prisoner either.*
>
> —Mick Jagger

The Future Is Uncertain

You might worry that the future is unclear and, like Sam, that everything has to be perfectly aligned before you're ready to move into it. If you do that, you won't start pursuing your next big thing because the foundation hasn't been anchored. This kind of approach to action couldn't be further from reality.

In fact, the future rarely comes to pass the way you imagined it. All you can really do is to know your past and choose the actions you take today which will move you closer to who you want to be in the future. They are laying a foundation for what you're intended to achieve in your lifetime. Are you ready? You are. You're exactly the person you need to be at this moment. Have the courage to take those steps necessary to successfully drive yourself to a more confident, more accomplished, and more forward focused you.

Personally, what has led me to embrace the unknown of the future is surrender. I believe that I'm being guided and that there is a bigger plan for me than I can even imagine. So I surrender to the moment and do what needs to be done to take a step forward. Generally speaking, our perspectives are very narrow. Having confidence that I am on the right course, trusting my instincts and faith that a higher presence is guiding me provides comfort as I progress into the vast unknown. When I start to feel apprehensive about the future, I tell myself not to look down and surrender to the moment.

> *The future is the home of our deepest fears*
> *and wildest hopes. But one thing is certain when it*
> *finally reveals itself. The future is never the way we imagined it.*
>
> —Shonda Rhimes

All You Have Is Now

We've established that the past is behind you. It only has the impact that you allow it to have over your present situation. We've also discovered that the best-laid plans can only estimate what lies ahead. Therefore, all you really have is this moment.

This is the time for you to focus on making the best of each experience and fully engaged in each day of your life. It's these moments that will shape who you are for the rest of your tomorrows. Whether you have just a precious few days or tens of thousands of them ahead of you, no one knows for sure. It's up to you to live each day as if there won't be another. As I sit to write this on May 1, 2021, I know there will never be another day like this one in all of creation. The value in my today is what I give it, and that is true for you too. So how do you squeeze each drop out of your day?

Make Every Experience Count

Don't take your experiences and activities for granted. Too many conversations happen while multitasking. We don't take the time to really hear the people we are talking to. Even if you've heard their stories many times, there's something unique in their emotions, expectations, and need for sharing the information this time. Listen carefully, and you can comprehend those things. Take this opportunity to listen actively, deeply hearing what they are sharing with you. This also helps to deepen relationships.

Avoid putting off tasks that will impact your life. They keep hanging around and taking up valuable real estate in your mind. Attack those tasks that are nagging your subconscious. This is a sure-fire way to move your life into a new, more positive direction. You'll feel like you're making progress and you'll be freeing your mind to focus on the next target once you clear the table of lingering tasks in front of you.

Do your task with joy and determination regardless of what they are. When you act with purpose and intention, it gives you a feeling of progress and accomplishment. Even if the work isn't done to the best of your ability, it's done. You can feel that steps are being made towards a more successful future. I know this is easier said than done. Often all of us, myself included, begrudgingly do things we'd rather not. Putting a smile on your face (happy that when you start you are closer to being finished) and charging through those tasks, you can feel more positive about the day and your victories within it.

Respond to the Inputs

Your actions and decisions might not always be the best ones for the situation and that's ok. If they're important, you'll have the opportunity to repeat ineffective choices in the future. These dilemmas will continue to present themselves to you in new contexts until you've completed the lesson. That's naturally how we learn: choices, evaluation, and correction. As a result, rather than waiting for the perfect timing or completely avoiding the situation, take some action instead.

Once you've acted, read the situation. Did you successfully move the needle, or is there a correction needed? At the next opportunity, respond with a new tactic. Don't worry, you'll eventually figure it out, and you will be wiser for the experience. Responding to what you see, hear, and feel will help you to have more success over time. Today, just taking action is enough.

If you take one thing away from this book, let it be that you have complete control over your actions, and thus your life. Yes, you and no one else controls your life. You may have little say over where you are but you have 100% control over what you do. While your natural tendencies are guided by your past, what you do today does not depend on what has come before. Today is a new day. The choices and actions you take are up to you. The responsibility for all your tomorrows rests on the accountability you have to yourself today. Don't take that lightly. Only you have the power to do what you are doing in this moment. Make the best of it, no remorse and no regrets. Win the day today, and let tomorrow take care of itself.

Destiny is no matter of chance.
It is a matter of choice. It is not a thing
to be waited for, it is a thing to be achieved.

—*William Jennings Bryan*

Tying It All Together

There is only one day you own, and that's today. Learning life's lessons and reflecting on the past will only help you so far as these things raise your awareness of how to do things better in the future. Likewise, the future is uncertain. You can't know with 100% certainty, what lies ahead. Find the courage you need to live the beautiful life you were meant to with the belief that you are moving in the right direction. Make the most of today. That is all you have. That is all any of us really has.

You can make the most of your day by being fully engaged in your activities, reading and responding to situations and your environment in ways that help you to be a better person today than you were yesterday. Live each day as if it were your last, doing everything to the best of your present ability. Then you will have no regrets. As the day comes to a close, you will have a quiet sense of confidence, knowing that you've given it your all. You will sleep with rapture.

Here are some exercises to help you focus on today

- ▶ What are some themes that continually present themselves to you?
  - ▷ What do you think you are supposed to learn from these?

- ▶ What is something you have anxiety about in the future?
  - ▷ What is something you can do today to reduce that anxiousness?

- ▶ What is your vision for your life 6 months from now?
  - ▷ How about a year?
  - ▷ Two years?
  - ▷ Ten?
  - ▷ What are some easy things you can do to move towards that vision?

- ▶ What is something you've been putting off?
  - ▷ When can you get that done?

- ▶ How were you successful today?

- ▶ What is a mistake you have made recently?
  - ▷ What have you learned from that?
  - ▷ How will you do better next time?

- ▶ Complete this sentence: I am proud that I accomplished _____ today.

▸ Now, look in the mirror and say it to yourself.

Get your free companion workbook for additional support at https://www.synergypersonaldevelopment.com/workbook/

18. Don't Compare

Whenever we evaluate our personal development, we often find ourselves in an underappreciated situation as we compare ourselves to others. There is no way to be satisfied with those results. There will always be someone better, smarter, and more skilled than you are. If there isn't, you're fooling yourself. Your experiences and time commitments are quite different from those of the people around you. As a result, where you see difficulties, others may see success. Thus, it is better to measure your success against yourself, not others.

Using yourself and your personal goals as the measuring stick of success allows you to more realistically chart your course. You can envision what comes next and the path to move ahead. You can also be more open to seeing others achieve what they seek and as a result be a propeller. You can then be appreciative of their success and offer praise for their well-done work. So how can you become more aware of your progress? It all comes down to three things; measure, communicate and sprint.

Set Quantifiable Goals - Measure

Setting quantifiable goals allows you to objectively measure if you are hitting the mark. These checkpoints can be evaluated with a yes/no answer. For example; run 3km twice during the week, use a new word you have learned four times in a day, or write 500 words every day for a month. Through use of these clear and specific goals, you can accurately monitor your progress in two ways:

First, you can readily understand if you have achieved your goal. Secondly, it is easy to track your progress. If you are using a system like lessons learned, which we will discuss in the next section, look back to discover opportunities to apply what you had hoped to and then do better next time. You may even try a three-step grading system: 1) Attempted, you made some effort to achieve the goal; 2) Competent, you succeeded but maybe it was luck or chance that made that possible; and 3) Confident, you can repeat the action smoothly and in a variety of situations. This grading process will give you clues into the next steps you'll need to achieve in order to reach your targets. Write down your perceptions and evaluations. That will quicken your start up time and help to motivate you when you next face a big challenge.

> *Success is not final, failure is not fatal:*
> *it is the courage to continue that counts.*
>
> —*Sir Winston Churchill*

Talk to Others - Communicate

As I mentioned in chapter 14, *Who Can You Turn To,* if you are having difficulty understanding how to succeed or your progress is slow, ask others who have cleared similar hurdles how they did it. This will provide you additional options for success that you may not have considered before. While their situations are undoubtedly different from yours, their approach may be a novel one that gets you over the hill.

Additionally, by talking to others about what you are working to achieve, you create a sense of urgency and accountability to make progress.

> *You should never try to be*
> *better than someone else,*
> *you should always be learning from others.*
> *But you should never cease trying to be*
> *the best you could be because that's*
> *under your control and the other isn't.*
>
> —*John Wooden*

Use the Scrum Approach - Sprint

Scrum is a project management philosophy that focus on achieving progress in sprints. These sprints have the goal of producing something that demonstrates progress over the previous version of the product or service. Software and engineering projects are often managed using the Scrum project management system. I love Scrum because it focuses on making progress in sprints that require demonstrated proof of concept and achieving success incrementally. More times than not, I turn my goals into projects so that I can effectively manage tasks, check progress and nimbly make adjustments.

If you are setting your goals too high you are probably also expecting to reach those achievements too quickly. Using the Scrum approach, you would consider what level of improvement would make a noticeable difference (maybe 5-10%) and how to achieve that. Once you have cleared that goal, work on the next big thing to move you forward to noticeable change, considering all the variables and task completions necessary to achieve that step by step. Just like the proverb says, *How do you eat an elephant? One bite at a time.*

Here is how I scrum personal development:

- ▸ What is the achievement I want to make?

- ▸ What are the tasks I need to clear to show noticeable improvement?

- ▸ Choose a task to move forward.

- ▸ Move another task forward.

- ▸ Repeat until all steps are cleared.

- ▸ Reframe the next visible achievement.

- ▸ Repeat the process.

> *How do you become better tomorrow?*
> *By improving yourself, the world is made better.*
> *Be not afraid of growing too slowly.*
> *Be afraid of standing still.*
> *Forget your mistakes, but remember what they taught you.*
> *So how do you become better tomorrow?*
> *By becoming better today.*
>
> —Benjamin Franklin

Tying It All Together

The only way to make true progress is to take it step by step. There are no shortcuts. Don't feel discouraged because someone else does with ease something you are struggling with. They struggled with it too, or something else, at some point. Just be ready to put in the work. Stay focused and celebrate your progress. Life is a marathon not a sprint, and you should run to complete the whole race, not just make it up the next hill.

Here are some exercises to help you make steady progress

- ▶ What is an achievement you want to make?
  - ▷ What are the tasks you need to clear to show noticeable improvement?
  - ▷ What is a single task you can do to move forward?

▷ What is the next task you need to do to move forward?
▷ Prioritize the remaining steps
▷ Repeat until you attain your goal

Get your free companion workbook for additional support at https://www.synergypersonaldevelopment.com/workbook/

Moving Forward

*N*ow that you have a firm understanding of yourself and what makes you tick, it's time to shed the past and move forward. In life we are forever growing or decaying. There is no middle ground. Which way your life goes is up to you. As long as you are reaching for something more you are growing. Moving forward and making progress is painful. It always has been, and always will be. To achieve a life you are proud of, you need goals and aspirations. We will plunge into those concepts and strategies here. You will learn techniques for creating and measuring your goals as well as methods for clearing the barriers that lead to a false sense of defeatism in the mind. And when you clear groundbreaking milestones, don't forget to celebrate a job well done before moving on to the next challenge.

19. What Is Your Fear Telling You

*A*s I walked out of my boss's office, one thing she said stuck in my mind above everything else, "We are downsizing, so your job and department are being eliminated."

What!? After spending my entire career getting to this position, one I really love, I am now being pushed out the door. I really had no idea what I was going to do. Afterall, I had invested most of my professional efforts into this company and building skills that allowed me to move up the corporate ladder. Now the rungs have been cut and I'm seeing myself slide down that ladder, like a terrified teenager experiencing the death of a thousand cuts in a bad horror movie.

Fortunately, I had the sense to invite my fear to lunch. We considered the past, did an inventory of the present and made a plan for the future. When our lunch was over, fear and I shook hands and went our separate ways. Your meeting with fear may not be so cordial. You may feel him taking a firm grip of your neck and heisting your hopes and dreams of a comfortable future from you before he departs. This doesn't have to be the case. You can find a way past fear. A method to develop lasting confidence and not just survive your travesties but actually prosper through transcendence of the experiences.

Prepare for the Battle

Often, you find comfort in the past, even a confining one. We each know our pasts, and they don't hold any surprises. As a result, we often come to believe that the past offers us stability. This is, however, not true. The past restricts. It limits your growth and stifles potential, because living within the limits of your previous potential does not offer you an opportunity to stretch the boundaries and metamorphosize into the most recent version of yourself. Challenge what frightens you and transform yourself through growth. That is how you will achieve a higher level of existence. You deserve a chance to experience that!

> *I learned that courage was not the absence of fear, but the triumph over it. The brave man is not he who does not feel afraid, but he who conquers that fear.*
>
> —*Nelson Mandela*

I am the kind of person that says yes first and figures out how to solve the problem later. While this has led to many difficulties, I always, yes always, come out of these situations better than I went in. Here is an example:

When I worked in the entertainment industry, my company won a big contract to offer a pay-per-view event to nightclubs, bars, restaurants, casinos and hotels across the United States. In fact, at the time

Mayweather vs. Pacquiao was the biggest pay-per-view event in history. This contract, however, required that we use a call center to handle the large volume of calls and orders we were expected to receive.

We were small, and no one had any experience in running a call center. I put up my hand and pledged to figure it out. By the day of the event, our call center was operating from three countries and had closed over $3 million, about 10% of the event's net, in sales.

Was it easy? No, I worked 16-hour days in the weeks leading up to that event. Was it fulfilling? Absolutely, I used my training, IT, project management and problem-solving skills to make the collaboration successful. We grow through what we go through.

Life consists of ups and downs. It is a series of peaks and valleys that bring you both joy and sorrow. Realizing that your existence is fluid and always changing will help you to free yourself from the obstacles that are holding you back.

Looking out over the horizon, you'll see a vast unknown. As a result, it is natural to gaze out into that void with anxiety and fear. Even though you are moving into uncharted territory, you are not doing it alone and unprepared. You have experience, skills and a network of people to help you through these trying times. You need to take inventory of your resources, plot out how to use them efficiently, and take action. This is your opportunity. Seize it and march into the future bravely, accepting your fears and finding a way to navigate a course beyond them.

> *One of the greatest discoveries a person makes,*
> *one of their great surprises, is to find they can do*
> *what they were afraid they couldn't do.*
>
> *—Henry Ford*

As you look at the road that lies ahead, you may have hopes and dreams of what your life could be. Maybe those ideals end with, "but someday," or "if only." This limiting self-talk blinds you to possibilities, and keeps you static in a rapidly moving world. Why not take a few steps down the road to see your future with better clarity?

Fear often causes us to become immobilized, unable or unwilling to take the next action. You may be apprehensive about your future. Maybe you feel that failure is inevitable, and there is no sense in trying to get beyond it. This may have you asking yourself, why even make an attempt? I'll tell you why. You deserve more and you can achieve it. You won't know what you are capable of if you don't make an effort. Dip your toe in the water and take some time to honestly evaluate the experience. This is the way to discover the solutions that work best for you. The reality is that for every person and in every unique situation, it's all trial and error, you have little to lose and so much to gain.

Don't be afraid of failure. Of course, you are going to fail, that is how we learn to succeed. Naturally, it won't be easy, nothing worth its weight ever is. Nevertheless, take the moment for all it's worth and wrestle your success from it. You are the master of your life, in spite of your fears and shortcomings. It is through this process of facing your fears that you will reduce apprehension and build confidence. As you build confidence, you will gradually begin to see that you are where you need to be at this moment, with the opportunity to do what you have been cultivated to do, in order to become the person you are meant to be. Don't hesitate, be brave and seize the moment.

I've learned that fear limits you and your vision. It serves as blinders to what may be just a few steps down the road for you. The journey is valuable, but believing in your talents, your abilities, and your self-worth can empower you to walk down an even brighter path. Transforming fear into freedom - how great is that?

—Soledad O'Brien

Accept failure as a by-product of the process. It is a chance to develop, become more intelligent, stronger and more prepared for the battles ahead. Failure does not equate to surrender - It is an indicator that you need to learn more. In that process you will realize how to succeed.

You don't yet have the benefit of hindsight, that usually comes long after the experience. As a result, you may not know the reason for the dilemma you are experiencing, what you are to take from it and how it can help guide you to a better existence. You need to complete your due diligence, have faith and jump. No regrets.

Make Fear a Colleague

Understanding your fears and what feeds them is vital to triumphing over them. We tend to fear what we do not understand, therefore learning about your fear and why you are experiencing it will help you to overcome the anxieties that accompany your strong feelings of apprehension and maybe even terror. This knowledge will better equip you to manage not only the situation, but also future dilemmas.

Examine your fears and anxieties. Learn to identify what triggers and feeds them. Then reflect on solutions for overcoming them. If you cannot find the answers within yourself, seek them out in books, mentors, friends, and other sources. In time, instead of looking for avenues of retreat, you'll be confidently proclaiming: "Been there, done that!" Chalking up victories big and small along the way.

This ability to face your fears head-on will eventually lead you to freedom. Freedom to stand up and be recognized as a person of value. Freedom to live life on your terms. Freedom to unleash the talents and abilities that have been locked inside you for too long. This all starts with looking your fears in the eye and considering the message they have for you. Fear is not a bad thing. It comes with a message; you need take action to move away from what frightens you. Whether you fight through the fear or circumvent it, you are the only one who can defeat your fears. Control them, or they will control you.

> *Being aware of your fear is smart.*
> *Overcoming it is the mark of a successful person.*
>
> —Seth Godin

Tying It All Together

This life is the only one you have. You can choose to peek through the peephole when opportunity, in the form of a problem or conflict, knocks at your door and lock the deadbolt. Or you can open that door and greet the experience with a firm and friendly, "Hi, how ya' doing!?" It's completely up to you.

Some common areas where we may find ourselves succumbing to fear are abusive relationships, work environments where we are taken for granted, or friendships that seem to be built on dependence. Believing that you are worthy of a more fulfilled life will unlock the potential to move away from those situations. It isn't easy, but when trouble knocks you down, get up and force a smile, then punch it right back. Accept nothing but the best from yourself each and every day, regardless of what defines your best on any given day. It's important to keep working at combating your fears. If you fall off the horse, get up and try again.

> *As we let our light shine, we unconsciously give other people permission to do the same. As we are liberated from our own fear, our presence actually liberates others.*
>
> *—Marianne Williamson*

Here are some exercises to help you manage your fear

- ▶ What is something you fear?
  - ▷ What is it about that situation that causes you anxiety?
  - ▷ What do you think that fear is trying to communicate to you?
  - ▷ How can you overcome that?

- ▶ What is a challenge you have been reluctant to take on?
  - ▷ How can you take action on that?

▶ What is an opportunity you want to challenge but don't feel you are ready for?
  ▷ What is preventing you from actin on that?
  ▷ How can you remove that obstacle?

Get your free companion workbook for additional support at
https://www.synergypersonaldevelopment.com/workbook/

20. Get Goal Orientated

When I was 26 years old, I began pursuing the dream of becoming a black belt in martial arts. After attending my demo lesson and receiving feedback from my instructor that it would take at least four years to achieve this goal, I went home and started a countdown on my calendar of the 1,500 days to black belt.

There were days, sometimes weeks, when I did not want to practice or go to the dojang. I had injuries and work commitments that kept me from attending classes, yet I never gave up. When I couldn't take part in class, I assisted in lower belt-level lessons. When my friends were having pizza and beer and enjoying a night out, I practiced my katas, or forms.

Short of finishing my bachelor's degree, which took eight years, working to achieve a black belt was the most challenging thing I had ever done. Near the start of my 6-month preparation for the black belt test, I quit my job. I had already missed the maximum number of days, 3, after only one third of the program. I knew continuing to balance these two demanding responsibilities would end in failure on both counts. In the end, I passed my test and became a black belt.

I don't practice martial arts now, but the lessons I learned about dedication, teamwork and determination still guide me to this day. If you were to ask my Grand Masters Jim L. and Bo Buhisan what the achievement of a black belt means to them, they would say a true martial artist wears their black belt around their heart. Being a role model and serving their community every day. I believe that too.

Somehow, I feel that if I hadn't earned my black belt, I would have been scarred for life. This feeling comes from the fact that before I earned my black belt I often came up short in achieving goals and had a tendency to give up on projects before I brought them across the finish line.

Achieving goals of any size will challenge you to dig deep and find a version of yourself that is inspiring, uncompromising and full of vigor. The way to awaken that person inside you is to set goals and attain them.

You may be skilled at setting goals and laying out plans. Perhaps, you are skilled at understanding how to achieve the ambitions your mind perceives, but slow to take action. Maybe you wait for the right conditions to get started. Perhaps you are quick to discover roadblocks that will make your journey difficult, if not impossible. If you are a chronic slow starter, there is no better time to set sail on your course than now.

What is it you've always wanted to achieve? Why do you want to achieve the goal? How will you transform your life by achieving that? Don't think this transformation is unimportant, through the process of working towards the achievement you will change for the better.

Stretch Goals

When you consider what is possible, set stretch-goals at double, triple or quadruple your intended target. Creating goals well above your limiting beliefs will help you to achieve more than you thought possible.

Expect setbacks along the way and to fall short of your expectations. That is normal. However, the stretch-goal will take you further in your ambitions and when you fall short, you may find you have already surpassed your original target. When you fall, get up, dust yourself off and continue on, knowing that what you just tried requires modification. There are many ways to achieve success. Experimentation is the surest way to find the course that is right for you.

> *Many people dream of success. To me, success can only be achieved through repeated failure and introspection.*
>
> —*Soichiro Honda*

While your goals may be high, the steps should be small. By moving towards the prize in small, incremental steps you can mark your achievement and feel a sense of accomplishment. This is the purpose of the belt system in martial arts. This incremental step process is so successful it is incorporated into other types of learning like music and process improvement. Likewise, you need to have some milestones worth celebrating.

> *Shoot for the moon and if you miss you*
> *will still be among the stars.*
>
> —Les Brown

Your path may diverge at one of those milestones as the journey to your destination changes and enters into uncharted territory. This is all part of the experience. You may need to add a new skill, or the path to your dreams sends you in a different direction from what you initially envisioned. Achieving milestones provides you a resting place, or plateau, to re-evaluate and re-tool for the next leg of your journey.

What's Your Why

The best way to ensure your success is to have a strong motivation for achieving your goals. Consider why you want to do what you are set on. My why in reaching for a black belt in my late 20s was to achieve more mental and emotional control of my life and an increased sense of wisdom. Those objectives presented themselves in the times I struggled. They were visible when I handled conflict in other situations and as I focused on providing more value in interactions with others. They still serve me today.

My whys for writing this book were to help you gain more control of your life through sharing tools and techniques that have worked for me, and to tackle my lifelong dream of writing a book that springboards me into new opportunities.

Your whys will be deeply personal. They will drive your decision-making process. They will keep you focused when you want to quit, and become the secret powers that drive you to achieve more than you thought was possible. They need to be strong and they need to be yours.

Writing this book took years of motivation to keep focused on my successes and failures, knowing that they would lead to something bigger. It also took a year of dedication to writing every week. Publishing articles that were the basis for these chapters, seeking feedback, continuing to improve my craft and then spending long hours at the computer compiling and editing all the drafts and versions. Motivation will get you started, and dedication will take you over the finish line. But first, you need to understand why you want to work so hard to achieve.

Your whys cannot be handed down or borrowed from someone else. They are part of your purpose for living. We will discuss this in more detail later. For now, focus on goals that align with the person you are, not one that has been created by your environment and other people. For example, getting a college degree or a high-profile job because that is what your parents want; or desiring a job with a big salary, so you can show off your status. These whys may leave you feeling resentful rather than excitedly challenged when times get tough.

If your whys are not inspiring you, it is common to want to give up at the first sign of adversity. If you feel that it is easy to get diverted, your why are not strong enough. You'll need to reexamine them and reevaluate your goals.

> *You need to overcome the tug of people against you as you reach for high goals.*
>
> —*George S. Patton*

There will be barriers to your achievement. Temptations will be standing by, waiting for you to stumble into the pit of unrealized potential. There will be time for pizza and beer when you have reached your goal. When you are on the path to growth, it's easy to backslide. When things are not going as you had anticipated, it is not uncommon to develop a case of stinking thinking, complaining that someone else has it easier or better than you do. During these times, you'll need to step back and refocus your efforts, doubling down on your success. You can succeed, one step at a time, be more encouraged by your steps forward than discouraged by your steps back. Stay dedicated.

One way to ensure that the distractions and barriers don't preclude your achievements is to create a list of rules and principles that guide your thought process and decision making. These rules will serve as a way for you to check that you are making progress and living with integrity to yourself. Some of my rules are: Always give my best effort, choose projects that help me to grow, and not to worry about the past but learn from it. With these rules, it becomes easier to make decisions about what steps to take next.

Creating a set of rules takes time and really requires you to consider your expectations. You also need to set clear boundaries to ensure that you do not get taken advantage of. *Fool me once, shame on you. Fool me twice, shame on me.* Create and revise your rules to develop into the best version of yourself. Live by them to strengthen your character.

There will be times that it appears you are on a collision course with failure. Don't worry. It is in these times that you develop resilience. You can quickly make some steps back up the mountain by repeating your past successes and learning from your previous failures. It's not always smooth sailing. You will learn the most during those stormy times. So, hold tight and get ready to grow.

You may think the skills you have or the achievements you have made are easy, and anyone could do that. This is simply not true. Achievement comes with hard work, dedication and sacrifice. You have to be willing to do the things others won't to achieve the things others don't.

Take pride in your accomplishments, enjoy a feeling of pride when you are able to do something that you previously thought was impossible. Feel a sense of joy that you have moved one step closer, and be diligent so that you will continue until you achieve what you have set out to accomplish. Plan and act now, but keep your focus clearly on the future.

Tying It All Together

Success does not come cheaply. You need to let the people and things that are holding you back go, so you can make space for insightful relationships and new experiences. Sure, it's scary and unknown, that is what makes it exciting.

The road to success will take you through dark places where you do not know what to expect and you will feel vulnerable. When adversity strikes, as it always will, you may find yourself more inclined to retreat than go forward. Don't. Meeting these challenges head-on will make you better, no matter the result. No one ever got better by winning all the time. To grow, you need to fail, learn, try again, and repeat, continuing this cycle until you find yourself winning, situation by situation. Appreciate every hard-fought victory, regardless of how small it may seem. When you finally achieve your goal, and you have reached the mountain top, don't forget to savor it. Marvel at what you have achieved. Relish it. Celebrate the victory. Enjoy your accomplishment. Then get ready to take the next challenge, which means starting again, but from an ever higher elevation.

Here are some exercises to help you be more focused in planning and going after your goals

- ▶ What is something you achieved that was difficult?
  - ▷ How did you benefit from that experience?

- ▶ What is something you learned from a previous failure?

- ▶ What is it you've always wanted to achieve?
  - ▷ Why do you want to achieve this?
  - ▷ How will your life be transformed by achieving it?
  - ▷ Write that as a goal.
  - ▷ Rewrite that goal as a 4X goal.

- ▶ What are the principles that are guiding you to achieve your goals?

- ▶ Write some rules for keeping on course.

Get your free companion workbook for additional support at https://www.synergypersonaldevelopment.com/workbook/

21. Chart Your Progress

*H*ave you ever felt that you're failing because things aren't going as smoothly or quickly as you had hoped? Whether your focus is on making it through the day or you have a big goal broken into steps, understanding your progress is critical to your success. You're achieving incremental steps, and sometimes clearing major milestones without even realizing it. Still, you're dissatisfied. So, how do you know if you're succeeding?

You Will Improve in the Areas You Measure.

To really understand your development, you need to have some metrics that help you to chart your progress. This is especially true when developing skills, like a foreign language or improving your presentations. Create metrics that allow you to quantify your success. Having measurable objectives will give you a clear understanding of your development. Here are a couple of examples.

I was working with a client on improving their ability to participate in meetings. As part of her annual review, Natsuko's boss told her that she needed to speak up more in meetings. "You have outstanding insights into the challenges of this project," her boss told her, "but you don't share those ideas in meetings, and that hurts the team's ability to grow."

Natsuko and I set a measurable way for her to be more assertive in meetings. We started with speaking out twice in a meeting (a quantifiable goal). When she only spoke out once, we examined where she had missed opportunities to engage. After she identified those and practiced some techniques for interjecting, she was able to offer up comments three times in her next meeting. We then focused on presenting an opinion, answering two questions related to her point, and paraphrasing information (her own or rephrasing others). Soon Natsuko's engagement surpassed even her boss' expectations.

When I practice guitar, I measure things like 1-minute chord changes (30), mistakes during a song (0), and the number of times I add a personalized embellishment (1) as ways to track my progress. Achieving these indices lets me know when I'm ready to move on to the next lesson. For you, the key is to choose some targets you can objectively mark as points of success.

The targets you'll track need to be quantifiable (objective) rather than qualifiable (subjective). Initial success is in the achievement, not the quality of the achievement. Additionally, you need a simple feedback measure to chart your progress. Did you achieve your target, yes or no?

The problem with creating a subjective feedback measure is that it takes too much effort for those of us who aren't behavioral scientists. What I mean by that is it requires time to build an effective feedback cycle. Subjective metrics rely on someone else making an appraisal of your efforts and deciding when it's good enough. Why give up that control? Most will agree that it takes more than 10,000 hours of practice to become an expert. Your skill will improve as you repeat the task in which you choose to grow expertise. As you reach 100 or so completions, you will notice a dramatic improvement from your initial efforts. So stick with it and don't give up. Very few succeed on their first try.

My guitar playing is getting better as my chord changes get faster. Natsuko is becoming a more effective communicator as she acts more assertively in meetings. You'll have more success too when you count the number of times you hit your objectives.

Lessons Learned

Once you have objective metrics for measuring your progress, you need to analyze your results. Have you succeeded? What were the reasons for that? Have you had setbacks? How can you overcome those? Analysis of success will help you to replicate your achievement. Analysis of setbacks will help you to adjust your course. They say that we learn more from mistakes than success. I firmly believe that. When you misstep, you discover alternatives through trial and error. That makes you more versatile and leads to future successes. Muhammed Ali said this about challenges; "You don't lose if you get knocked down; you lose if you stay down."

These questions will help you to make steady progress:

- ▶ 7 Questions for setbacks?
    - ▷ What are the problems I'm having in clearing this?
    - ▷ How can I overcome those?
    - ▷ Was there a specific point where I consistently hit a roadblock?
    - ▷ What was that?

▷ Am I lacking some ability, piece of knowledge, or a skill that will make this easier and give me a clearer understanding of the situation?

▷ Did I miss an opportunity to apply the skill I'm developing?

▷ What could I have done to take advantage of that opportunity?

▶ 10 Questions for success

▷ Why was I finally able to clear this milestone?

▷ Is there something about the process that is duplicatable?

▷ What am I capable of now that I wasn't 3 months ago? 6 months ago?

▷ Do I need to reassess the next phase(s) of this journey now? When do I need to reassess?

▷ What's something that was unexpected?

▷ What's next?

▷ What other skills/knowledge do I need to develop?

▷ Who contributed to my success?

▷ Have I told them?

Asking and answering questions like these helps you to assess where you are and where you're going. This analysis will give you a bird's-eye view of your situation. That will enhance your understanding of what should follow and the resources you have at your disposal for the next challenges.

Next Steps

Now that you have evaluated where you are, it's time to make some adjustments. You have more knowledge and experience than you did when you started. Based on that, are your strategies still viable? Is your next step still the same? Reassess before you move on. This will help you to move forward more smoothly and have greater success not just with the next part of your life's journey but further down the road, too.

Once you've reassessed, it's time to recommit. Know that this journey makes you more skilled, more knowledgeable, and more agile. Find joy in and celebrate what you've achieved so far. Then ready yourself for what comes next, commit to success on the next leg of your development. You've made it this far, get excited about the next stage of your growth.

Tying It All Together

Achieving your goals, whether consecutive days getting out of bed or becoming a skilled public speaker, is a process. To ensure you're making headway, you need to measure your success in quantifiable ways. Make sure to set targets that are easy to calculate (E.g., number of times you did X). Through evaluation, you will identify patterns that either lead to your success or get in the way of it. Then you can make the necessary corrections to get on the right track. Once you've evaluated your situation, raise your finger to the wind, take a deep breath and confirm that you are moving in the right direction. Then recommit to your success.

Here are some exercises to help you more effectively chart your progress

Questions for setbacks

▸ What are the problems You're having in clearing this objective?

▸ How can you overcome those?

▸ What was a specific point where you consistently hit a roadblock?

▸ What ability, piece of knowledge, or a skill are you lacking that will aid your progress?

▸ Did you miss an opportunity to apply the skill you are developing?

▸ What could you have done to take advantage of or to perform better in that opportunity?

Questions for success

▸ Why were you finally able to clear this milestone?

▸ What about the process is duplicatable?

▸ What are you capable of now that you weren't 3 months ago?

▸ 6 months ago?

- ▶ Do you need to reassess the next phase (s) of this journey?

- ▶ When do you need to reassess?

- ▶ What's something that was unexpected?

- ▶ What's next?

- ▶ What skills/knowledge do you need to develop next?

- ▶ Who contributed to your success?
  - ▷ Have you told them?

- ▶ Do you need to adjust your goals or targets?

- ▶ What is the next step?

- ▶ Map the rout to the next observable point of progress

Get your free companion workbook for additional support at https://www.synergypersonaldevelopment.com/workbook/

22. Celebrate Your Victories

When was the last time you succeeded at something? I am not talking about a big achievement; I mean just moving the pile forward.

We often take our victories for granted using self-talk like, "It's no big deal," or "Anyone could have done that." However, these achievements are worth celebrating. As you progress towards your bigger goals, make new achievements and embrace novel experiences, taking some time to congratulate yourself creates positive imagery that helps to generate more success.

Formulate and stamp indelibly on your mind a mental picture of yourself as succeeding. Hold this picture tenaciously. Never permit it to fade. Your mind will seek to develop the picture... Do not build up obstacles in your imagination.

—Norman Vincent Peale

As you make progress and perceive achievements, you may find it easy to forget that you were not always as nimble and skilled as you are now. The advanced skills you have acquired may seem easy now, but it took time to develop those. Experiencing achievers' amnesia may result in you forgetting how you struggled and felt that you would never add the new skills and abilities you have worked to develop. Now that you have the aptitude and the altitude, you may feel that everyone else can do those things with ease, too. This is a fallacy that could lead to trouble when setting expectations for both yourself and others. By celebrating your accomplishments, you add memories and positive images that will serve you well down the road when you consider how you got to where you are and help you to avoid achievers' amnesia.

I remember when I was about 6 or 7 years old, and I looked down and thought to myself - *It is kind of far from here to the ground.*

Looking at your achievements and life progress with wonder helps you to appreciate all that it has taken to get where you are. You realize and appreciate what you are capable of accomplishing if you put your mind and heart to it. Therefore, never lose sight of what it took to achieve that goal, whether it is one you achieved in a day or that took several years to realize.

Recognize your milestones with a clear vision of where you want to go and what you want to achieve. Doing this enhances your ability to visualize the achievements and major accomplishments. Taking some time to praise your efforts at those points will propel you to the next stage of the journey with enhanced enthusiasm and motivation as you see your dreams turning into reality.

When you struggle with something and finally succeed, there is a big difference in how you will view challenges in the future depending on your response to finally getting over the hump. If you say something negative to yourself such as: "Why am I so slow to figure this out, I must be really dumb," you are attaching negative thoughts and energy to new challenges, making you want to avoid them, and pushing the prize further from your grasp.

On the other hand, if your self-talk is positive and sounds like: "Wow! I can't believe I was able to do that. It is such an awesome feeling," then the next time you encounter a new challenge it will be a lot easier to overtake. Using the power of positive self-talk you are going to attract more success and feelings of self confidence to clear any hurdle you face.

When I speak Japanese, sometimes my brain and mouth seem disconnected. My brain knows what to say, but my mouth says something different. Rather than get frustrated, I take this as a sign that I am making progress and consider what I could do to get those guys working together.

As you become more self-assured and achieve more wins, don't forget about those who have had a hand in your success. Those propellers that cheered you on, the people that gave you insight to a new way of perceiving the problem, and even those pessimistic folks that said you could never achieve what you set out to do. They all gave you motivation in one way or another. Don't forget to update them on your progress and say thank you for their contributions. That helps to build your gratitude muscle.

You can achieve all the things you want to do, but it's much better to do it with loved ones around you; family and friends, people that you care about that can help you on the way and can celebrate you, and you can enjoy the journey.

—John Lasseter

Rewards Are Helpful

Whether you are intrinsically or extrinsically motivated, promising yourself a reward for achieving a milestone is a reminder of the journey and a celebration of conquering the challenges. For extrinsically, or externally motivated people, knowing the reward that awaits you at the end of the journey may help you to persevere for longer than you would have otherwise. Intrinsically, or internally motivated people, will find that the reward is the proud feeling that stems from looking back on the challenges you've overcome and realizing your accomplishments on the road to your eventual success.

One of my mentors, wealth and prosperity coach Randy Gage, often decides what the reward will be in the preparation stage of a new project. For example, he may decide that when he finishes his next book, he is going to get a piece of art for his home; or when his speaking tour is complete, he is going to get a new car. Then when times get tough, he has another focus beyond the grind of completing the task. The reward that awaits.

> *I think it's important to celebrate your successes.*
> *It's important to feel happy about them, but it's equally*
> *important to look forward to the next big move.*
>
> —*Chanda Kochhar*

An alternative way to set rewards is not fix the reward in your mind until you are nearing the finish line. Then, when you complete the significant goal, make a day of rewarding yourself.

For example, If I am going to buy new pair of athletic shoes, I will spend time researching the brands, colors, prices, etc. Once I have decided, I will take myself to lunch before or after going to the store. I will spend time talking with the salesperson and really making the reward an event worth remembering. Maybe I will also get some new clothes for the gym. Those things help me to feel that my accomplishment brought me an extraordinary experience.

You don't have to wait for the major accomplishment to reward yourself. Treating yourself to a moment of pleasure or gratitude with a smaller reward for a job well done or a barrier knocked down is effective too.

Tying It All Together

Once you have accomplished something, grown to new heights or crossed a developmental threshold, it is common to forget what it took to get there. You may expect that you should achieve these new targets every time. That just isn't true. Development includes peaks and valleys and sometimes you will need to unlearn something to do it better and achieve greater success the next time around.

Celebrating your victories is a way to capture your achievements and move those successes into your long-term memory. Honoring your triumphs and recalling the hurdles you overcame will create good feelings around your victories, and the reward will help to make those results tangible, preparing you for the challenges that lie ahead.

These precious moments where you celebrate your victories will serve as later reminders that you can do what you set your mind to. Take a moment to pat yourself on the back for a job well done and give yourself a little reward as a way to say, *I have achieved something special.* Celebrate your achievements as something spectacular and you will never forget that they were special.

Here are some exercises to help you celebrate your success

▶ What is something you do with ease now that was at first a struggle?
  ▷ Explain a situation where that skill or ability failed you.
  ▷ Explain a situation where that skill benefitted you or another person.

▶ What is a reward for achieving a goal you are working on?
  ▷ Describe how your life will be impacted by achieving this goal.
  ▷ Visualize that moment for a few minutes before going to bed every night.

▶ Who had a hand in achievement of a recent milestone or goal?
  ▷ How could you thank them?

Get your free companion workbook for additional support at https://www.synergypersonaldevelopment.com/workbook/

23. You Will Win When You Learn to Embrace Your Hardship

A few months ago, I started learning to play the guitar. Over that time, I've made some progress. I can now play rhythm for some cool songs and also use different strumming patterns on occasion. Am I good? No, I wouldn't say my playing impresses anyone except me. I don't expect to be able to play any Queen or Pat Metheny covers for quite some time. No worries, I want to enjoy playing guitar for the rest of my life. Not just impress my friends tomorrow. Another student said this the other day, "You'll succeed at playing guitar as long as you don't give up." I couldn't agree more.

Not giving up is the key to success that this book presents to you. You can achieve anything you want in life if you choose to stick with it. Too often when we face our first real challenge or feel that we're not making fast progress, we decide that pursuing our goals is no longer worth the effort. That's a shame.

When you start to acquire a new skill, you will see huge improvement at the beginning. This happens for two reasons: First, you have no skill or very little of it at the start. Secondly, you're excited, so you pour a lot of energy and enthusiasm into growing. This momentum can't last over the long run. You'll need to have other motivations to keep progressing, such as strong whys and rewards to help you get through the tough times that will be inevitable as your journey continues. Don't give up on your dreams, you have envisioned them because they are now, or will be over time, within your reach.

> *If you're going through hell, keep going.*
>
> —*Winston Churchill*

The Journey to Your Goals

Over my 20 plus years of teaching and coaching, I've seen that developing any skill or ability is similar to walking a mountain range. You'll start by going up one mountain. Then you will have to descend to challenge the next one. As you climb towards the peaks you will reach plateaus. These high flat points are good places to check your progress. You won't want to stay there forever, or you will never reach your destination. Up and down, over hills and into valleys. Some of it is beautiful and other parts are treacherous. Persist and you will begin to feel proficient. As you continue on your journey, you'll realize that there's no end in sight. The further you go, the farther there is to go. Development is infinite.

You may feel this infinity in your despair as well, but making small incremental steps moves darkness out of the valley and replaces it with light. As I stated in the last chapter, count your wins no matter how small.

When you're working towards a big goal sometimes you will have success. At other times you'll feel that you're not making any progress. Then there will also be times when you feel that you're backsliding. Don't worry, it's all part of the process. If you're making your best efforts, you're winning.

> *Just as a gardener must tend his or her plot, keeping out the weeds, you must tend the garden of your mind, weeding out the thoughts of lack, limitation, and negativity. You must nurture and tend the thoughts of happiness, success, and purpose.*
>
> —*Randy Gage*

Embrace the Difficulties

If you're a grinder, like me, you love the difficulties. A grinder is someone who sees the goal ahead and pushes forward like a bull in a china shop to achieve that. Most people aren't grinders though. When times get tough they find it easy to slip back into familiar patterns and undesirable habits. If that's you, stop. It's time to see difficulties for what they really are, tests of endurance and motivation. Difficulties and roadblocks are the places where you'll have the most development. When you clear these obstacles, you'll have a whole new perspective on your road ahead. At the end of the day, growth is painful but yields gains.

You don't necessarily need to keep pushing that rock up that steep slope. Sometimes you need to take a step back. Do an inventory of where you are, what you know, what tools are at your disposal to utilize and make a new strategy. Talk to someone about your progress and challenges. You'll get a fresh perspective by explaining the situation to them. You will also gain valuable insight you may be missing due to being too close to the situation. Nothing is impossible if you embrace your difficulties and consider how you can overcome them.

As part of his training, a karate student was told by his master to move a huge rock. The rock, in fact was as large as the student himself. The master assured the student that he possessed the tools needed to succeed.

First the student pushed the rock but it would not budge despite exerting all his strength. Then he found a rope and tied it around the boulder and tried to pull it from its place without any luck. Next, he picked up a board lying nearby and tried to use that as a lever to move the rock. Still he did not have any success The student thought and thought about how to move that rock, but in the end, he decided it was impossible.

He reported this to his master, who replied, "you have not used all your tools."

To which the student again explained his story again. The master then responded, "you did not ask me."

How often we overlook the most obvious tools we have for solving our most difficult challenges.

Difficulties test your motivation for achieving what you're working on. Weak motivation will have you giving up at the first hardship. Strong motivation will allow you to withstand any challenge that gets between you and what you want to achieve. So make sure that your whys are strong partners. You're going to take those "whys" with you in good and bad times all the way to the achievement of your goals. They will be there to remind you that you haven't reached the destination yet, so keep going.

> *You may encounter many defeats, but you must not*
> *be defeated. In fact, it may be necessary to encounter the defeats,*
> *so you can know who you are, what you can rise from,*
> *how you can still come out of it.*
>
> *—Maya Angelou*

Play the Long Game

As you move along your path adversity will strike, guaranteed. Time-bound goals are effective for business. However, in your own life, you'll be better off adjusting those deadlines. Realize that arriving at your destination weeks, months or even years later is still an achievement about which you should feel great pride and sense of accomplishment. It's better to arrive at your destination later than hoped for than not arriving at the goal at all. Here is an example from my own life: My musical journey started in middle school and seemed impossible until only a few months ago. This book is also a project more than ten years in the making. Give yourself a break. If you can see the target, you can achieve it.

Life is a marathon, not a sprint. Consider that whatever you're doing now is getting you closer to where you want to be, so long as you aren't spending all your time sitting on the couch binge-watching TV. Keep that project, desired results, and goals in the front of your mind. Experiences and opportunities will aid your development and progress. It may take longer than you'd envisioned, but with determination, you'll get there.

Have you ever had the experience of hearing a song you needed to hear at precisely the right moment, randomly opening a book to a prophetic piece of wisdom or being given an opportunity to develop a skill that is the next needed ability for your journey? If you have, then you know that what you need manifests itself, coming into your life when you need it. Making what you want to achieve a lifelong commitment will unlock many doors for you, you just need to be open to hearing the directions. Consider your development as a journey of endurance - little by little, like Aesop's turtle, you will win the race.

Only you can do what your mind and spirit are telling you to do. You've got to carry that torch and make your life one of achievement. No one else can do it for you. When you're feeling down and like your life is meaningless, you've got to find some internal drive to shake that off and move forward, believing that you have value and untapped potential.

You have a purpose. You're unique, and there will never be another you on this planet. Challenge the life you have and continue reaching out for the one you want. Break those expectations that are holding you back and create new ones that will catapult you forward. It doesn't matter how old you are or what you've accomplished in your life so far. You're destined to make a difference in the lives of others, the health of the planet, or some other contribution that's aligned with the person that you are. With thinking like this, your feelings of despair and hopelessness will occur less frequently, because you are filling your mind with positive thoughts and feelings of prosperity. When those overwhelming negative feelings do come, you'll have developed the weapons and talents to keep them at bay initially and eventually maybe even kill them off completely.

Tying It All Together

It's through growth, learning new skills and acquiring knowledge, while unlearning misconceptions, false ideas, and inefficient processes that you can conquer the mental and psychological blocks that are holding you back. Day by day through vision, determination, and persistence you will find little victories that provide rays of hope and lead to bigger ones. Just don't give up on yourself.

Here are some exercises to help you break through your hardships

▸ What is something that is holding you back?
  ▷ How can you move beyond it?

▸ If you could change one thing in your life what would it be?
  ▷ How can you do that?
  ▷ Over the next couple of weeks, what are some steps you could take to make the change?

▸ What is a negative memory you'd like to erase?
  ▷ What could you replace it with?
  ▷ What are you doing to achieve the vision of yourself you see in your mind's eye?

Get your free companion workbook for additional support at https://www.synergypersonaldevelopment.com/workbook/

24. Delay Rewards

*H*ere are stories about two of my friends. Which one is more like you? My friend Paul is impetuous. He sees something he likes, and he instantly finds a reason to reward himself with it. If he wants to go out to dinner on Wednesday night for example, he justifies it to himself by saying, "I closed a deal today, so I'll treat myself to dinner."

Emma, on the other hand is prudent. She sets goals and adds rewards for major accomplishments. Emma started playing guitar. She bought a used and serviceable instrument for $50. She considered buying one that cost ten times that amount. She told herself that if she studied for a year and completed the 26-lesson beginner's course, then she would buy a guitar that she really liked, regardless of the price. Emma finished her first year of guitar and will go guitar shopping this weekend.

If you can create reward systems like Emma's your motivation will be longer lasting and the success you achieve will be more memorable. Delaying gratification allows you to fully appreciate the gifts and experiences that are part of your everyday life.

Grabbing for those experiences and objects that are right in front of you without thought to consequence can lead to a feeling of emptiness in the end. This emptiness comes from needing more in order to feel adequate. That dopamine high from the excitement of the moment is good, but it's short-lived.

> *Hey, Mummy... I've decided I want a squirrel!*
> *Get me one of those squirrels!*
>
> —*Veruca Salt (In Ronald Dhal's Charlie and the Chocolate Factory)*

We all want that quick hit of pleasure, that immediate entertainment or the decadence that a delicious dessert brings. You want it and you want it now. How much better would the experience be if you had a more substantial connection to those rewards?

In the famous Stanford Marshmallow Experiment, Dr. Walter Mischel offered children a treat now or two in 15 - 20 minutes. Some children ate their treats immediately. Others squirmed in their chairs, distracting themselves by singing a song, or chose to move away from the table entirely in an effort to avoid looking at the marshmallow in hopes of scoring two.

In the end, most children caved. The ones who didn't received a greater reward. As teenagers, they were also found to do better on standardized tests, and as adults, they had more successful careers. Mischel concluded that children who were able to delay their gratification generally become more self-reliant, self-confident, and less distractible adults. They also proved to be more able to cope with stress and anxiety as adolescents.[1]

---

1 Mischel, W., Shoda, Y., & Rodriguez, M. (1989). Delay of Gratification in Children. *Science, 244*(4907), 933-938. Retrieved June 28, 2021, from http://www.jstor.org/stable/1704494

While it may seem that the ability to delay gratification is a trait folks are born with, it can absolutely be developed. It's a form of patience and patience can certainly be practiced and honed. Like Emma, you can teach yourselves to wait, and in doing so have deeper experiences and an increased sense of value for your accomplishments.

> *Delayed gratification is a sweet lesson whose teacher knows the best is not right now, it is yet to be.*
>
> —Maximillian Degenerez

Choose Instant Motivation Over Instant Gratification

When you choose immediate rewards over more substantial long-term ones, you inevitably leave value on the table. You may experience slowed growth or even a lack of development since you never really got to test what was possible. This creates a "just enough" mindset, doing "just enough" to get by.

Paul uses this method of celebrating just enough accomplishments, and as a result he is never completely satisfied. His accomplishments are short lived and rarely build on one another. He often feels empty and desires to have more. While Emma is content with the progress she is making. She knows that continuing to focus on the big picture will help her overcome the challenges she is facing now, such as quick chord changes, and give her perspective to overcome obstacles, such as faster tempo songs with multiple chords changes and varied strumming patterns, in the future.

"Just enough" does not serve you well when you continue to fix the same problems over and over again or when your wins are superficial ones. Anxiety is often caused by the misconception that we have no time or other options available. This could not be further from the truth. Dig deeper and be more reflective to be an effective problem solver. You can learn to do this by taking some time to consider how you could do it better. We often think we don't have the time to be thorough and do excellent work. However, doing the task right from the beginning will save you time in the long run. Consider the tools and abilities you have learned over your lifetime and ponder alternative solutions that use your unique abilities before you begin. This will help you to remain calm while you work through the process, even if you need to make changes along the way. Going slow and being thorough results in the realization of wider long-term benefits later. This is a tradeoff that is beneficial almost every time.

Rewards are a good motivator. They help keep us focused on the prize, providing extra extrinsic value for accomplishment. Using them creates, as Emma does, a feeling of patient anticipation in achieving what you set out to do. If your progress is delayed, the reward will still be waiting at the milestone, ready to be collected.

When I am feeling distracted, having the promise of a later reward gets me to focus more on achievement. This helps me to move forward with a bit more joy and determination about achieving my tasks, especially the ones I'd rather not do.

The Joy of Anticipation

Everyone likes receiving packages, regardless of whether they are gifts or something you ordered. Choosing when to open the package allows you to create the emotional space for the joy of unboxing. If you give yourself this extra time, you will also have the opportunity to be completely focused on the experience.

Select a time to interact with these things when you can give them your undivided attention. Come to think of it, this is also a good strategy for engaging on social media too as you will avoid writing impulsive and often regretted responses. Allowing yourself to be completely engrossed in the experience for a few minutes will give you time to absorb the moment. Sit with it, ponder it, feast your eyes on the contents and prepare for the experience, then reflect. This kind of engagement will have a longer-lasting effect. It will increase your excitement in opening the package and your perceived value of the contents within it.

It's like a kid waiting to open presents on their birthday, enjoying each and every gift. As adults, we rarely get to experience this kind of excitement. Being able to manifest those positive emotions through your own actions is pure bliss.

One key to delayed gratification is being able to create a feeling of persistence. With persistence you suspend excitement in the moment to experience a rainbow of emotions that you slowly and deliberately reveal over time. This kind of self-discipline makes you better able to cope with emotional highs and lows. It is a kind of emotion training that enhances your ability to separate feelings from actions.

You can work in creating this persistence by giving yourself breaks when you have completed tasks, giving yourself micro-rewards like a short walk, gaze out the window, a snack or engaging in some other change of pace activity once you've completed a taxing task.

Persistence can also help you to manage anxiety. It does this by changing your focus from what is happening now to a longer view of how solving a problem now, or forging a plan to solve a problem that cannot be immediately resolved, has a clear benefit later. When you are feeling anxious about a challenge, take a step back and create other solutions, viable or not. Then justify the use of each one of these as well as the previous steps you've taken to solve the problem. This will help you to more clearly define the challenge and discover effective measures for overcoming it.

> *As we get past our superficial material wants and instant gratification, we connect to a deeper part of ourselves, as well as to others, and the universe.*
>
> —*Judith Wright*

Tying It All Together

All too often we want to experience things immediately instead of waiting for a time and place to more thoroughly engage with them. When you delay rewards, the gratification of the experience is often more fulfilling. It provides the opportunity to enjoy a variety of emotions. Delaying gratification usually results in better rewards, because the benefits often grow with time. An additional benefit of delaying gratification is that it trains you mind to apply a clear separation between feelings and actions in positive situations so that you can better apply this self-management skill in times of distress.

Here are some exercises to help you delay gratification

▸ Forego small rewards for bigger ones.

▸ What are the rewards you will receive for achieving success on your present goals?
  ▷ What are some small rewards you could give yourself (I.e., taking a walk in the park or a TV timeout) for achieving milestones throughout the day?
  ▷ What are some milestone rewards you could award yourself for greater progress?

▸ What are some ways you could push yourself a little harder?

▸ What is a big reward you could give yourself for a major accomplishment?

Get your free companion workbook for additional support at https://www.synergypersonaldevelopment.com/workbook/

Creating Good Habits

*Y*ou have become more aware of who you are and built a stronger relationship with yourself. Hopefully you also have a clearer understanding of your environment and how to manage it. These tools will help you as you move forward. Now, in order to sustain that development and make those new processes stick, you need to build routines and habits that create a foundation of living the life you desire every day. This foundation will support your emotional weight have you winning more days than you lose, having the confidence to keep up the fight when it appears that things are not going your way, and to rise above your fears and inhibitions to experience a life you will be happy that you woke up to every day. Good habits will keep you focused on how to effectively manage yourself and your life every day.

25. Developing Positive Rituals & Habits

"Watch your thoughts, they become your words; watch your words, they become your actions; watch your actions, they become your habits; watch your habits, they become your character; watch your character, it becomes your destiny."

—Lao Tzu

What you do every day makes you who you are. Oftentimes you may not be aware of the actions you perform regularly. Those are quite often accomplished unconsciously. As a result, it may seem as if your life is on autopilot. To combat this and make changes in your programming, be more conscious of the things you do. Take control of your habits, the singular actions like the way you eat or how you brush your teeth. Create effective rituals, the groups of actions you do, at the start of your workday and before you go to bed at night. By crafting grounding rituals, you will reshape your life into one more of your choosing.

Using Habits to Create a New Structure

Usually, when you want to change your life, you will immediately look to add a fresh habit or two, such as exercise or changing your diet. Then after three days, three weeks or three months, you find that you have quietly abandoned those recently added actions. You give up, even though you knew these new activities are good for you. You may now feel they present a burden to continue, or that you have failed in your attempt to change and cannot face the challenge anymore. That is absolutely understandable. It happens to all of us. What I have found works for me is to consider exchanging old habits for new ones.

First, to gain a new habit let go of an old one. Multitasking on changing habits is one of the most strenuous exercises to accomplish. Instead, choose a habit that you want to get rid of and one you want to develop and pair them. For example, If I wanted to give up smoking (I am an ex-smoker) because I know it is not good for my health, even though I enjoy the moments of relaxation I derive from puffing on a cigarette. I reason that smoking makes me feel calm and in control, if even for a brief time (recall the discussion of the benefits of delaying gratification). However, I also know that I smoked because I have a high level of stress. Then a friend suggested I practice meditation to help me quit smoking, I discovered a way to achieve the desired result of reducing stress but with a different action. So, if every time I wanted a smoke, I instead did a five-minute mindfulness meditation, I could effectively manage my stress and not damage my health. In fact, it would take no longer than smoking a cigarette did in the past. Now I have a new tool for stress management, meditation, and it will be easier to give up smoking one day and meditation session at a time.

As I become more consistent in my meditation practice, I can incorporate that habit into my day in other ways. For example, I could make it part of my morning routine or the thing I do before going into a high-pressure meeting. Little by little, my negative habit of smoking will be completely replaced with the more beneficial one of meditation.

It is important that you assess your habits in the same way.

▸ What habits do you want to eliminate or adjust?

▸ Which new ones do you want to welcome into your life?

▸ What is one thing you could change in your day-to-day life that would have a dramatic impact on your outlook and personal development?

These questions will help you to see your habits for what they truly are. The underlying foundation of your life.

Using Rituals to Deepen Your Personal Commitment

Rituals are a series of actions you may use at set times throughout the day (i.e., a morning ritual or a get home from work ritual) or in conjunction with other activities, like giving a presentation or getting ready to go out on a date. These groups of actions can have a great impact not only on your present mindset but also your future results, making it easier (or more difficult) for you to create desirable outcomes. What are the actions you do in the first 30-60 minutes after you wake? How do you psych yourself up before a big meeting? Do your rituals need a fine-tuning or a complete overhaul?

The first step to managing your rituals is to understand them. You will be able to see them more clearly by documenting them. Before bed, play back the day in your mind, like a movie. Notice the ritualistic actions you perform and document those by situation (I.e., before leaving the house or at the end of your work day). Continue journaling every day for a week. The patterns of your unconscious actions will slowly begin revealing themselves to you. Once you understand your rituals, you can begin making adjustments to them one habit and action at a time. You are probably saying to yourself, "But John, several of these habits have to go!"

That may be true, but you don't want to overwhelm yourself or shock your mind with a major change. That could devastate your progress. Instead, take it one action at a time. Like a cook perfecting a recipe or a marketer looking to increase engagements, if you change too many things at one time, you won't know which of the changes was the one that made a difference. Go slow and stay results orientated. Once you have dialed in one ritual, work on another. Consider this process a constant maintenance program. Before long, you will achieve the outcome you desire.

In essence, if you want to direct your life, you must take control of your habitual actions.

It's not all about talent. It's about dependability, consistency, and being able to improve. If you work hard, and you understand what you need to do, you can improve.

—*Bill Belichick*

How I Improved My Productivity

I used to go to work and pick up where I had left off the day before, reading and actioning email. Then prioritizing the day's tasks and continuing with a few breaks, meetings and responding to those email notifications whenever they popped up on the screen. Then I developed two new habits: Scheduling the next day at the end of the previous one and only doing email three times a day. These habits completely changed my work processes.

By scheduling the next day before I left the office for the night, I departed with a clear mind, not bringing physical or mental work home. I knew that I had a plan. As a result, my mind was free to focus on other things once I left the office and be present for those in my personal life Then when I got to the office the next day, I could quickly get up to speed on the agenda I had set for myself the night before.

The same was true with email. Doing email three times a day instead of everytime a notification appeared on my desktop helped me to turn avoid distractions. That allowed me to work longer and smarter on the activities that required my attention. Multitasking declined and my productivity soared just by changing these two habits and creating some new rituals. You can do that for you too, once you know what is standing between you and your success.

Tying It All Together

Recognize the actions that make up your day. Then, consciously build rituals that give you more control over your life. It is widely reported that upwards of 40% of our daily actions are habitual. Increased awareness of what you do and making mindful choices in how you do it will help you to feel like you are managing your life instead of it managing you.

Here are some exercises to help you create more effective habits and rituals

▸ What is a habit you want to eliminate?
  ▷ What is a new habit you could exchange it for?

▸ What is one thing you could change in your day-to-day life that would have a dramatic impact on your outlook and personal development?

▸ Reflect on the rituals in your life and log them.
  ▷ Note any adjustments you would like to make in different parts of the day
    ◆ When you wake up
    ◆ Before leaving the house
    ◆ To start your workday
    ◆ Before lunch
    ◆ After lunch
    ◆ At the end of your workday
    ◆ Before you start your evening commute
    ◆ When you first get home
    ◆ At dinner
    ◆ After dinner
    ◆ Before bed

Get your free companion workbook for additional support at https://www.synergypersonaldevelopment.com/workbook/

26. Live Each Day to the Fullest

*I*n a recent interview, iconic songstress and business tycoon Dolly Parton told the world she starts her day at 3 am. 3am! By the time the clock hits 7, when many of us are just waking up and rolling out of bed, she has already finished her prayers, daily meditation and completed 3 hours of writing. If she's not eating breakfast by that time, she is in the kitchen preparing it. Dolly's morning routine may seem unbelievable. But you too could achieve more, and bring increased levels of success into your life by waking up a little earlier and living each day more fully.

There are countless books and programs for creating effective morning rituals. Many successful people have meticulous morning routines, and, unless you are the rare bird that finds structure suffocating, you can stack up a large number of wins throughout the day with effective rituals. When you start devising your morning routine, you should create one that allows you to feel a sense of balance and helps you to record wins every morning. These activities will give you a sense of accomplishment that will make the start of your workday feel like the middle and bedtime seem like a victory lap.

Every day I feel is a blessing from God.
And I consider it a new beginning.

—Prince

If you find it hard to get out of bed in the morning, try using 3 alarms. Start by setting the third alarm. That one is for the time you will get up. Then set the two others at fifteen-minute intervals before that.

In the morning when the first alarm goes off, pray, meditate, do positive affirmations, or state what you are grateful for. Anything that gets you in touch with your spiritual self and helps to ground you is fine. If you prefer to do this from the comfort of your bed, that's perfectly ok, too. If you doze, no worries. Just focus on spiritual connection in that first fifteen minutes.

Alarm two is time to wrap your head around what you need to accomplish for the day. At this point, your mind will be a little sharper. Visualize your day and the list of things you need to do. If you have a presentation or important meeting, visualize yourself not just succeeding at that, but thriving. In your visualization, you own the room and everyone is in awe of your level of knowledge and input. If you are a student, imagine yourself answering every question correctly on a test or stunning your seminar group with your depth of knowledge.

When you visualize success, you are less likely to feel disrupted when things don't go as planned or worse - reel out of control. You will be more prepared to handle these problems because you have already created positive momentum in your mind.

Alarm three is time to roll back those covers and jump out of bed, ready to win the day.

It's not fun to get out of bed early in the morning.
When the alarm goes off, it doesn't sing you a song: it hits you in
the head with a baseball bat. So how do you respond to that?
Do you crawl underneath your covers and hide?
Or do you get up, get aggressive, and attack the day?

—Jocko Willink

The First Promise of the Day

The first promise you make to yourself every day is to get up at a fixed time. When you break that promise, you start the day with a loss. It's sometimes difficult to rally past loss number one, and as a result, you may seem to have no momentum throughout the day. Instead, set yourself up with an easy victory. Plan to get up 30-60 minutes before you have to. This time will give you space to take charge of your day.

Oftentimes, waking up late will result in you chasing the day. When this happens, it's very difficult to feel a sense of control or to realize that you have had any level of accomplishment. On the other hand, getting up early allows you to create a flow to the day and notice its rhythms.

I usually wake up at 5 am, and by the time I am preparing for work at 7 I've had a relaxing cup of coffee, read a few pages of a book, completed my prayers, and finished exercising. By getting up early, I am able to see patterns in my morning that help me throughout the day.

If I over-pour my coffee or drop a plate, it is a sign to pay a little more attention to the small details throughout the day. Likewise, if my morning goes smoothly, without much focus on how to do the tasks, I know I need to trust my instincts more. They will guide me through. There are signs of the rhythm and synchronicity to your day too. You just need to have mental space in your morning to comprehend those signs, and that means going about your routine methodically and leaving yourself the time to do so.

Lose an hour in the morning, and you will spend all day looking for it.

—Richard Whately

Whether you are working on a big project or just getting your day off on the right foot, starting with a win or two helps you to be more positive. One easy way to stack up victories is to knock down tasks that you are working to being consistent in performing. This may include exercise, writing, or reading a few pages of a book. They can also be avoidances such as not watching or listening to the news (it tends to be on the negative side), not hitting the snooze button, or not using social media before work.

No matter what, or how many, wins you achieve in the morning, your day will go smoother if you can tick any off of your list. These achievements create a positive, upward spiral that will provide you momentum for moving effectively and being resourceful throughout the day.

Get up every morning, tell yourself you are beautiful,
and gear up to win!

—Manushi Chhillar

Sometimes, however, things just don't go as planned. There will be days that your morning sucks and nothing goes as planned. It happens. You don't have to accept that your day will be miserable. Instead, behave yourself into a new reality.

While emotions and memories are strong, actions are stronger. If you don't like the direction your day is taking, change your mindset, and change your actions. Emotions are one way your body and subconscious communicate with you. To improve your emotional state, analyze what that message is, and make the appropriate move. Thinking and responding, rather than feeling and reacting.

You may not be able to control your emotions, but you can manage your actions. Choose to do those things that move you in a more affable direction.

I get up every morning and it's going to be a great day.
You never know when it's going to be over,
so I refuse to have a bad day.

—Paul Henderson

After You Turn Out the Lights

As you lay your head on your pillow, reflect on your day, your successes and shortcomings, also consider your discoveries and surprises. As you run through the story of what was, count your victories, and analyze what you could have done better in areas you suffered disappointment. What lessons did you receive today? How can you apply those to your future?

Doing a daily inventory like this will help you to feel a sense of achievement for the day.

You may not have been as successful as you had hoped, but you have moved forward from the person you were yesterday. Regardless of if you have taken a step forward or back, resolve to make tomorrow better than today, utilizing the knowledge and experience that has come from this day. Consider what is on your agenda for tomorrow and resolve to give a good effort as a means to achieving success at those tasks.

Just as you did in the morning, visualize your success. Finally, spend your last waking moments dreaming. Dreaming of what you want your life to be. Creating this vision of the future will sprinkle seeds of success along your path. If you fall asleep, that's perfectly ok. Maybe you'll overcome your challenges and move closer to the life of your dreams as you sleep.

Above all, before you go to bed each night, make sure you have squeezed every last drop out of the day. Tomorrow is not promised. So you need to get as much out of each day as possible. When you go to bed exhausted, besides falling asleep quickly and sleeping deeply, you will also have a real sense of accomplishment. If you didn't accomplish all you wanted to, it certainly won't be for a lack of effort, and hopefully, you'll have tomorrow to continue working your plan.

Even if I ain't the famous-est, the richest, the best -
as long as I know I kept it real and didn't backstab nobody -
I sleep good at night.

—*21 Savage*

Tying It All Together

Waking up early and going to bed exhausted will help you feel you have won the day. Winning life a day at a time means you mount victories in the coming weeks, months, and years too. You were born to succeed. Starting and ending your day with reflection and a solid plan will help you to achieve that.

Here are some exercises to help you live every day to the fullest

- ▶ Create your 15-minute spiritual routine.

- ▶ What are you going to accomplish today?

- ▶ What is your thrive visualization?

- ▶ What promises did you make to yourself today?
  - ▷ Did you keep them?

- ▶ How can you keep tomorrow's promises?

- ▶ What did you achieve today?

- ▶ If you had setbacks, what were they?
  - ▷ What can you learn from them?
  - ▷ With hindsight, what would you have done differently?

- ▶ What lessons did you receive today?

- ▸ What is a victory you had today?

- ▸ How is today better than yesterday?

- ▸ How will tomorrow be better than today?

Get your free companion workbook for additional support at https://www.synergypersonaldevelopment.com/workbook/

27. Unlock Your Self-Control with Meditation & Mindfulness

*O*ne problem that I have with managing stress and anxiety is getting my mind to slow down. It sometimes seems to go a thousand miles a minute. Sometimes my mind will project the impact of a mistake far into the future or create overly imaginative visualizations of the activities in front of me. These mind dialogues often lead to confusion about what to tackle next or doubt that I can achieve what I really want.

Information overload has very little, if any, value. The results are usually an overly inflated ego about my importance and the success of my work, analysis paralysis caused by a lack of self-confidence, or an inability to prioritize tasks successfully. There is no middle ground. It is either all wonderful or a complete disaster. A couple of ways I have found to combat these feelings are meditation and mindfulness.

Meditation

Meditation is the age-old technique of slowing your mind and focusing your attention. It helps to untangle the threads of thoughts that are dominating your consciousness and distracting you from making real progress.

During meditation you focus your attention, weakening the effect of jumbled thoughts that may be crowding your mind, and producing stress. This process can result in enhanced physical and emotional well-being. It has for me.

To become skilled at meditation, you need to start with two rules: 1) Don't be critical of your ability to practice meditation. It's a skill and will need time to develop. 2) Continue to practice so that your meditation skill becomes a tool you can use to combat stress, reduce anxiety, and create positive self-talk. Meditation is a foundational tool for managing emotional well-being as well.

Here are some meditation techniques that I frequently use. Hopefully you'll find one that is a good fit for you.

Guided Meditation

This is a good way to begin the practice of meditating. Guided meditations have a narrator or speaker talking you through the meditation process. There is often soothing music playing in the background. You can either sit or lie down and close your eyes. You can also do gentle movement with your eyes open like Tai Chi or just swaying from side to side. Then just do as instructed in the audio or video program. Don't worry if you fall asleep. Your subconscious is still hearing the meditation and you will realize some positive effects after the practice is completed.

Prayers & Chants

Using prayer is a good way to quiet your mind. You focus on the words and images that are part of the prayer. This takes your mind away from those troubling thoughts that may be overwhelming you. Instead, you focus on the mystic elements of the prayer. Buddhist chants, mantras, The Lord's Prayer, and Rosaries are common prayers for this kind of practice. There are countless books of prayers that you could use to enhance your spiritual energy.

Like with guided meditation, you don't need to invent your own to use prayers and chants. You need only read, listen, or memorize these, then repeat them to feel their power. I like prayers because I sense that I'm deepening my spiritual relationships as I recite them.

Chakra Meditation

This is a more advanced technique, but there is no reason not to try it if using chakras resonates with you. The chakras are the primary energy centers of your body. There are seven of them, from bottom to top: root, sacral, solar plexus, heart, throat, third eye, and crown. Having these seven energy centers working in tandem helps life to go smoothly. However, if you have a blockage in one or more areas, you may be feeling that nothing is going right for you and your life is out of sync.

I often assess where a potential block exists and use a chakra meditation to clear it. If you are not sure which chakras to work on, you could use a meditation for all seven, or a guided meditation for just the lower or upper chakras as a way to start. My Reki master, Hazel Pardinas-Kennedy suggests to work on one chakra each day of the week as you learn about them.

Lower Chakras

Root Chakra

The root chakra is responsible for your sense of belonging. Its focus is on survival, security, safety, and family. If you are having financial challenges or feeling over-reliant on others, your root chakra may be the cause. When your root chakra is in alignment, you will feel self-confident and able to face life's challenges. It is located in the tailbone region of your body and its color is red. Sones like rubies, garnets and rose crystal will help balance your root chakra The sound that you can produce in meditation to focus on your root chakra is Uh as in cup.

Sacral Chakra

The sacral chakra is the base of your emotional wellbeing. If your sacral chakra is in balance, you will feel more creative and could have more sexual energy. If it's not, you may be experiencing difficulty in your romantic relationships. You may also be overly emotional or not feeling connected to others. The sacral chakra is just below your belly button and its color is orange. Power stones like orange sapphires, fire opals and sunstones can help you achieve balance if you feel that your sacral chakra is over or under active. The sound that strengthens your sacral chakra is Oo, as in you

Solar Plexus Chakra

If you are feeling overwhelmed or nervous about a situation, your solar plexus chakra may be the problem. Its focus is on inner strength and self-esteem. If this chakra is balanced, you will feel uninhibited and confident in expressing who you are and what you want. The solar plexus chakra is located just below your rib cage, and its color is yellow. The power stones that enhance your solar plexus chakra include amber quartz, topaz and citrines. The sound that helps you focus on your solar plexus chakra is Oh, as in go

Heart Chakra

Love flows through the heart chakra. It's the link between the lower chakras of the body and the upper ones of the mind. An open heart chakra allows you to feel love for yourself, those around you, and people in general. If you have a healthy heart chakra, you will experience a deeper sense of empathy, forgiveness, and compassion. As its name implies, the heart chakra is located in the center of your chest, and its color is green. Stones that are beneficial for the heart chakra include jade, emeralds, and green serpentine. The sound that activates your heart chakra is Aw, as in saw

Upper Chakras

Throat Chakra

The throat chakra is your center of communication. If you're feeling that no one understands you or that you're not communicating your thoughts and ideas clearly, your throat chakra may be the culprit. This chakra is also associated with timing. Feeling lucky? Your throat chakra is clear. The throat chakra is located in the center of your throat, and its color is turquoise. Some stones that will help to enhance the power of your throat chakra include turquoise, aquamarine and tourmaline. The sound that helps to balance your throat chakra is I, as in my.

Third Eye Chakra

The third eye chakra is your key to illumination. When it's healthy, you will find that your intuitions are accurate. You may have a heightened sense of morality and awareness of the world around you. If you feel that you can't catch a break or like your efforts are falling flat, your third eye chakra may be out of alignment. The third eye chakra is located between your eyes at your eyebrow line. Its color is purple. Stones like amethyst, lavender quartz and tanzanite enhance your third eye. To awaken your third eye chakra chant Ay, as in say

Crown Chakra

The crown chakra, located at the top of the head, plays a key role in your ability to connect spiritually. A person with a strong crown chakra can feel their connection to the universe and a higher sense of consciousness. This person will experience the beauty in themselves and the world around them. This chakra is often beyond our consciousness, as there is much to experience and learn before we can truly understand our individual connection to the universe. Still, it is worth attempting to tap into. The crown chakra's color is white or violet. The stones that will help bring out your crown chakra awareness include scolecite, clear quartz and moonstone Chanting or singing Ee, as in me will help to strengthen your crown chakra.

To practice chakra meditation, listen to the corresponding chakra frequency (you can find many of these meditations on YouTube) while sitting in a relaxed position. Focus on the area of the body that the chakra targets or form an image of the chakra's color in your mind. You can also do this while laying down. You may also want to create a more immersive experience by uttering the sounds as you exhale. I find doing this a few times makes me feel calm and confident. These frequencies will also be used in guided meditations. They are often part of musical pieces specifically designed to unlock and realign your energy forces. Chakra health is a focus of Reiki and Yoga as well.

Mindfulness

Another exercise I like for regaining a sense of control over my life is to practice mindfulness. Mindfulness is an exercise that involves being in the moment and avoiding distractions. One benefit of practicing mindfulness is that you are hyper-focused on what you're doing, where you are, and what you're experiencing. Here are some techniques for being more mindful.

Quiet Your Mind

Sit in silence, listening to, and experiencing your environment. What are the sounds that you hear? How does it feel to have the sun on your back or the wind in your face? Is there something baking in the oven? How does that smell?

Really be engulfed in your surroundings. Do this for as long as you can keep your focus on the moment. Once your mind starts to wander, stop. At first, you may only be able to quiet your mind for a moment or two, but as you continue to practice, your ability to focus will get stronger and you will gradually be able to sit in silence for long periods of time.

Single Task Focus

As you work through your day, choose some activities to do uninterrupted. No notifications, no distractions, just you and the activity. Keep your mind focused by scheduling the activity and when you feel your concentration slipping, remind yourself that you just have a few minutes to go until you take a break or move on to a new activity. I find that when I am focused in on just one task, I am significantly more productive. You may be too.

Be the Observer

Sit in a public place, like a coffee shop or park, and just observe the world around you. No judgments, just observe. So many people in a shared experience, yet each one is completely different from the others, like snowflakes.

How do people interact with one another and the environment? What are people wearing? Are they moving fast or slow? Just this practice of observation will help you to develop your own awareness.

Tying It All Together

Most of the time your stress or anxiety is self-generated. You do this by overthinking or not taking action. This is normal. Nevertheless, it's not going to increase your confidence or provide you an opportunity to grow your coping skills. Practicing meditation and mindfulness allow you to slow down for a few minutes and quiet your mind. With a new sense of calm, you will be more resourceful in your problem-solving. Having a greater understanding of your energy, emotions and environment. This enhanced consciousness will also help you to identify imbalances that you can repair with practice, resulting in living your day-to-day life with an enhanced sense of perception and control.

Here are some exercises to help you improve your mindfulness

▸ Choose a meditation and practice it for a week.
  ▷ What meditation technique did you use?
  ▷ Was it helpful (why/why not)?

▸ Try other meditations noting their effectiveness until you have 2-3 that you like.

▸ Sit quietly for as long as you can before your mind starts to wonder
  ▷ Record the time
  ▷ Continue this practice until you can sit for 15 minutes.

▸ Use this mind clearing activity to reset between tasks

Get your free companion workbook for additional support at https://www.synergypersonaldevelopment.com/workbook/

28. Healthy Life = Happy Life

*J*t used to be that when I got swamped in life, my diet shifted dramatically from rice, veggies, and chicken breast to burgers, fried foods, and snacks. This is the worst thing I could've done. Living on fast food; chili dogs and Taco Bell bean burritos with green sauce and extra cheese lowered my productivity and increased my mood swings. Combining that with missed doses of thyroid medication, and eventually I found myself checked in for a vacation at a mental health hospital.

I've applied a few basic strategies for health and nutrition since those days, and as I get older it becomes clearer that nutrition is something that makes a huge difference in all aspects of life and shouldn't be taken for granted. There are three ways that nutrition is vitally important. First off, what you put into your body has a dramatic impact on your performance. Secondly, health is the most important thing we have. Finally, a variety of foods is better than the same foods prepared the same way over and over again. If you're feeling sluggish, moody, or lacking inspiration, your diet and attention to health are probably partially to blame for that.

Garbage In Garbage Out – *For Your Mind Too!*

If you work in IT or data analysis, you're probably familiar with the expression *garbage in, garbage out*. This means if you put low quality information in, you will get low quality output. This is also relevant to diet: putting junk into your body will negatively impact your performance. This is one of the reasons top athletes choose lean meats, organic produce, and avoid filler ingredients in prepared foods.

Being a top-shelf professional athlete is not the goal of most of us here, but we can take a strategy from their playbook and make healthier choices. COVID KOed my walking habit. I went from 10,000 plus steps per day to less than 100 on a busy day. That meant that I needed to adjust my diet accordingly. When I didn't, I gained 20 pounds. 20 pounds!

I'm no doctor, but I know it's better to snack on protein bars, cucumbers, and carrots than potato chips, candy and cola. We would all benefit from taking more control of our diets, focusing on what we eat (and drink), and when we do so. If fast food sinks like a lead balloon in your gut and makes you feel sleepy, then you should resist that craving until your day off. Instead, spend more time cooking meals that are healthier and tasty, too.

I find that eating less of high-quality food is more satisfying than consuming a big cheap meal. After eating a nutritious lunch of vegetables and a protein lightly fried in sesame or olive oil, I'm more ready to conquer the afternoon than surrender to the sofa. Whole and organic foods are a much better choice than processed ones as well.

This technique can be used for indulgences as well. I enjoy drinking craft beer, India Pale Ale (IPA) is my favorite. However, if I don't have one in the fridge, or can't find one to my liking, then I'd rather drink water. Having guidelines about what you put into your body and setting parameters for what is and is not acceptable, helps to increase your sense of self-worth.

The next time you are trying to decide what to have for lunch, say to yourself - I deserve the better option. Then, choose it. For me, that means preparing my own meals more and eating out or getting something fast and convenient less.

Health = Wealth

When you are sick, life feels stagnant. It's hard to move forward because that takes too much energy. Yet, you don't want to slip back, because you have hopes and goals to achieve. Understanding your health scale and what's possible within it is vital for you to realize a sense of accomplishment. Everyone has limits. Those with severe illness are well aware of their boundaries. This allows you to avoid surpassing the red line of over-exhaustion. Those of us who are healthy either often don't challenge ourselves enough or push ourselves foolishly beyond the breaking point. Neither of these extremes is beneficial.

Regardless of your level of health, find a way to understand when your peak productivity times occur and how your diet plays a part in prolonging those. Experiment with different types of foods (E.g., beef, chicken, pork, eggs, or tofu as protein sources). Then, make incremental changes in your diet that move you closer to your personal peak performance. No matter how great or small, any forward momentum is significant.

Health is the single most important asset you have. Those of you fighting chronic pain and long-term illness are well aware of that. The rest of us take our good health for granted until we lose it. Instead, we all, regardless of health condition, need to take a more active role in our dietary choices.

Did you know that one way to bring out more vibrant colors in tropical fish is to vary their diets? Well, what's good enough for the fish in the aquarium is good enough for you too. Different colored foods have different nutrients and will make you more vibrant, just like those tropical fish. Eating a rainbow of foods helps. In her book, *The Rainbow Diet: A Holistic Approach to Radiant Health Through Foods and Supplements*, Dr. Deanna Minich states - not only are there benefits from the distinct nutrients found in different colored foods, but they also have a divergence of energies associated with them depending on the colors, and these correspond to the Chakra colors:

▸ Red foods are beneficial for combatting physical issues in the body (I.e., apples, cherries, and red bell peppers)

▸ Orange colored foods help creativity to surface and serve your emotional health (I.e., pumpkin, carrots, and oranges)

▸ Yellow foods enhance intellect (I.e., bananas, ginger, and grapefruit)

▸ Green foods benefit the heart (I.e., lettuce, kale, and cucumbers)

▸ Aquamarine foods are helpful for speaking and communication skills, in addition to thyroid health (I.e., sea vegetables like nori, hijiki, and wakame)

▸ Indigo foods unlock your intuition (I.e., eggplant, prunes, and blueberries)

▸ White foods open your spiritual connections to something beyond yourself (I.e., onions, coconut, and cauliflower)

Stimulating your other senses through food is also important. Food does, after all, satisfy your emotions as well as your body's need for nutrients. Your sense of smell is one of the strongest, just a whiff of miso soup makes me think it's breakfast time in Japan, while the smell of toast, bacon and eggs transports my mind back to California. The scent of grilled chicken in the air takes me back to summer picnics and softball until the sunset. These images that food is a catalyst for are not only personal but also cultural.

Choosing foods with pleasing aromas gives you a sense of comfort and wellbeing. While foods with odors that bring back memories of troubled times may be best to avoid altogether, or at least to prepare in a new way. If you find foods that have a Jekyll and Hyde effect on you, it may be a good idea to pay a visit to a psychologist to work through that trauma.

Tying It All Together

It is easy to think of food as just fuel that allows you to get through the day but being more intentional about your relationship with food will help you to be healthier and happier. Eating a variety of foods makes mealtime more interesting. Whether you're mixing up your food routine, adding new recipes, or enjoying cuisine from all around the world, a diverse meal routine enhances your joy at mealtime. I often say that the cook gets to enjoy a meal twice. Once while preparing it, and again when they are sharing it.

Occasionally, getting outside your food routines and making rules about what you will and won't allow into your body play a huge part in stimulating your mind, senses, and self-worth. No matter how delicious or nutritious your meals are if you eat the same foods every day you're missing out on a wider variety of essential nutrients and the benefits those foods unlock.

Here are some exercises to help you raise your diet awareness and improve your nutrition

▸ Fill your plate with as many colors of food as possible

▸ What colors do you need to add more of to your diet?

▸ What foods are those colors?

▸ Find a cooking website you like and experiment with new recipes.

▸ What are 2-3 sugar-heavy foods you can remove from your diet?

▸ Avoid eating 2 hours before bedtime.

▸ Keep a food journal and analyze the effects foods and their quality have on you

Get your free companion workbook for additional support at https://www.synergypersonaldevelopment.com/workbook/

29. Find Yourself Through Nature

*I*t's easy to get absorbed in the day to day of your life. You get up, go to work, come home, do your evening routine, and then it's time for bed. Do this over and over, and soon you'll feel as if you're just a cog in the machine. This is amplified when the view from your window is a concrete jungle, your commute is typified by trains packed to the breaking point or traffic jams that go on for hours. There must be an escape from that insanity, a way to be more connected and alive.

No matter where you live, there's most likely nature nearby: a park, some trees or your own garden. Experiencing nature provides an opportunity to recharge your batteries and ease your nerves. In fact, there are so many benefits to getting out in nature that making it a part of your weekly routine is essential to creating and maintaining good mental health.

Connecting to nature will help you to refocus, relax and re-align yourself to who you are and your greater purpose. After all, you are more than just a cog in the machine that gets a day or two of rest before you have to go out and do it all over again.

According to a 2019 study by Matthew White, getting out in nature for as little as a couple of hours each week can have powerful health benefits. Those benefits include: reduced stress and anxiety, better physical and mental health, and increased cognitive power. No special skills required. Just get outside and experience nature around you.[2]

About 10 years before this study came out, my video podcast, *Relaxation Media* provided viewers a few minutes of calming nature and simulated being outdoors. I believed then, as I do now that experiencing nature even virtually, has healing qualities. The podcast ended up becoming the #1 video podcast for wellness worldwide with thousands of downloads of each episode. It seems others agreed with me.

Today you can put on a pair of VR goggles and become immersed in a nature experience that's so realistic your brain will actually believe you are outside. While this is a good way to reset, it's even better to physically explore nature in your own area. Smell the trees, the grass, and the flowers. Hear the different bird calls and the gently flowing stream, if your park or recreational area has one. Even watching people play with their dogs and children will help to bring about a feeling of serenity.

Here are seven activities you can do to regularly connect with nature:

Mindful Observation

Sit on a bench or somewhere that you can be still for some time. Then, just watch your surroundings. Listen to the

2 White, M.P., Alcock, I., Grellier, J. *et al.* Spending at least 120 minutes a week in nature is associated with good health and wellbeing. *Sci Rep* **9**, 7730 (2019). https://doi.org/10.1038/s41598-019-44097-3

sounds and tune into the smells around you. Experience it all. You don't need to analyze or think about anything. Just be in the moment, a living part of the habitat. Breath deeply and experience the feeling of being connected to the environment.

At first, this will be extremely difficult. You may be able to mindfully observe your surroundings for only a few moments before reaching for your phone, wanting to take a picture, or otherwise disengage from the situation. Keep practicing and soon you'll be focusing for 5, 10, 20, even 30-minutes at a time, just you and the nature surrounding you.

As I was sitting on a park bench one afternoon, three lizards, a large spider, a centipede, and five different kinds of birds all stopped by to visit. These are things I never would have experienced if I'd had my face in my phone or been walking. Sitting still and letting nature come to you will reveal pleasant surprises.

Blind Immersion

For this exercise, close your eyes and let your other senses guide your experience. What do you hear? Is it approaching or receding? Which way is the wind blowing? How does the air smell? Touch the ground and just experience it, don't label it. Just feel. This heightening of the senses brings back memories of simpler days of playing in the park and letting my imagination run free. I hope it does the same for you.

Forest Bathing (Shinrin-Yoku)

In this Japanese practice, all you need to do is take a walk in nature and immerse yourself in the environment. Notice the terrain, plants, and wildlife you encounter as you walk. As above, soon you'll have a sense that you're connected to the environment surrounding you. That feeling provides both power and serenity.

Explore a New Natural Area Near You

If you are well acquainted with one park or natural area near you, look for another one that is close by. Set a date and time to explore this new area. That can make it feel like you're going on a new adventure. What's even better, if you have a friend that also likes being out in nature arrange to meet them there. Then you can enjoy the outdoors together. This is a great opportunity to strengthen your bond.

Sketch

Regardless of your artistic ability, sketching requires you to really observe your subject to capture its essence on paper. Whether you sketch the landscape, or the grass under your feet. Drawing your experience will help you to connect to nature and aid your ability to experience a personal relationship with your surroundings.

Journal About Your Outdoor Experiences

If you don't like sketching, you can also do a bulleted journal about what you're observing in your outdoor environment. How do you feel when you're outside? What animals, insects, plants are you seeing? Are you seeing any people regularly? You may be inspired to write poetry or explore other creative outlets while you're in nature, too. Many of the greatest poets, writers and musical artists throughout history were inspired by nature.

Observation Over Time

If you visit the same spot on a regular basis, you'll begin to recognize subtle changes. Noticing the differences from month to month and season to season is an experience you'll carry with you for a long time. That recognizable ambiance is something that you can recall through meditation whenever you need mental or emotional realignment.

Tying It All Together

Touching nature will increase your peace of mind, and it only takes a few minutes a day to engage with your surroundings. Whether you head to nearby open spaces or out to your own backyard, taking some time to connect with nature will help you to understand yourself and your environment in ways that are engaging and empowering.

Here are some exercises to help you strengthen your connection to nature

▸ Tend to your houseplants and/or garden

▸ Where are 3 places within a short walk or drive that you can experience nature?

▸ What are your 3 favorite nature spots?

▸ Add a visit to one of these to your calendar

▸ Easy nature experiences covered in this chapter:
  ▷ Mindful nature observation
  ▷ Blind immersion
  ▷ Shinrin-Yoku (forest bathing)
  ▷ Sketch or paint in nature
  ▷ Journal or do creative writing in nature

Get your free companion workbook for additional support at https://www.synergypersonaldevelopment.com/workbook/

30. Transform Your Life With Sweat

J don't know about you, but whenever I start the day with exercise and breaking a sweat, the entire day just seems to go a little bit better. While this is easier said than done, breaking a sweat first thing in the morning does have its benefits. Don't give up though, just because you miss a day or exercising in the morning is not possible. Breaking a sweat, even one day a week, is better than not at all.

Just by doing a little exercise, you will reap rewards. Some benefits beyond the physical ones include detoxification, improved respiration and circulation, increased endorphins, and enhanced energy levels. Breaking a sweat is also good for your mental health. With so many benefits, why don't we average Joes and Janes do it more?

It seems to me that one of the primary reasons we put off exercise or omit it completely from our routines is we do not think of exercise as being fun. If the boring routine of exercise is keeping you on the sidelines, make it a game of beat the clock, exercise to your favorite music, or choose activities that stimulate you such as playing sports or doing martial arts. There are virtually thousands of ways to get your heart rate up and your body moving.

You may also feel that you do not have time to go to the gym. If that is true, exercise at home. Exercise is a simple activity with a direct relationship between time invested now and the dividends you receive, both in the short and long term. The perks you can expect to receive far outweigh the pain of getting physical for a few minutes a few times a week. I do not know anyone that wants to be sick or unhealthy. Do you? One way to ensure that you are healthier is to break a sweat. Whether you are a couch potato, a busy mom, or a cancer survivor, getting in a workout of any length will help you be more fit mentally and physically.

It Can Be Simple

My base exercise routine takes about 10 to 15 minutes and is something easy to do at home. I start with 25 pushups and then do 5 minutes of planking. I added 50 squats to expand my program. Simple and effective. I notice the results immediately, and the boost in my energy level is more than apparent. No matter how many pushups, planks or squats you can do, working with a trainer to develop a routine that is right for you is a good investment in yourself.

Other do-at-home exercises like sit-ups or crunches, lunges, and jumping jacks, or even the dreaded burpee all use your body's weight for resistance to get your heart rate and breathing levels up while burning calories. Want to work on a specific area, or create your own routine? Just search for exercises that fit your needs, such as reducing tummy fat, increasing stamina or simple stretching exercises you can do at home. In Japan a short exercise program on public television network NHK called *Radio Taiso* shows simple exercises that can even be done sitting down. Start simple and add repetitions and activities as your routine becomes easier. This is a good start to getting your daily dose of physical activity.

Gold medals aren't really made of gold. They're made of sweat, determination, and a hard-to-find alloy called guts.

—Dan Gable

Exercise requires many of your body's systems to work in tandem. Starting your day with these systems in harmony will help your days to go more smoothly. Alternatively, exercising at other times of the day is good for getting into sync when you need a readjustment. Take your circulatory system, for example; exercise gets your blood pumping faster, and that moves the blood through your body with increased speed. This exertion also enhances your breathing rate, adding more oxygen to your blood and increasing its quality. Since a healthy brain circulates 750 ml (about a bottle of Jack Daniels) of blood every minute, that increased flow of blood and oxygen also helps improve mental alertness and state of mind. According to the Primary Care Companion to the Journal of Clinical Psychiatry, regular exercise improves self-esteem, reduces anxiety and feelings of depression.[3]

It's not even about looking good; it's about feeling good inside.

—Brie Bella

---

3 Sharma A, Madaan V, Petty FD. Exercise for mental health. Prim Care Companion J Clin Psychiatry. 2006;8(2):106. doi: 10.4088/pcc.v08n0208a. PMID: 16862239; PMCID: PMC1470658.

How Do the Japanese Live So Long?

The life expectancy in Japan is among the highest in all the world, with a combined average lifespan of over 85 years for men and women. That is a full six years more than people in the US, and a few more years than folks living in the UK and Canada. So, what is their secret?

One thing that surprised me when I came to live in Japan, over 20 years ago, was the high level of health consciousness compared with people living in the US. Here in Japan, people walk A LOT. Every morning people walk to the station and to the office, then repeat this process on the way home. I even see many of my silver-haired neighbors out walking every day.

They say that walking 10,000 steps a day, about five miles, is the key to a long and healthy life. I know from personal experience that my weight is lower and my energy higher when I get in those 10k steps regularly.

It will take me about 90 minutes to do that if I were to do it all at once. However, you can add a bit more walking to your day and before you know it, you will be moving more than you ever imagined. Here are some ways to increase your walking time:

▶ Take public transportation - Walking to and from the bus stop or train station like we do in Japan.

▶ Park at the far end of the parking lot, or even at one that is a little way from where you are headed - You can probably get in a few extra hundred steps each way with this strategy.

- ▸ Walk to the store - Is there a supermarket, drugstore, or beauty shop within a mile of your home? Why not walk there instead of taking the car?

- ▸ Walk your neighborhood - Just taking a 20-30-minute walk around your neighborhood will not only help digest your dinner but also have you understanding a bit more about the place where you live. You may even meet some of your neighbors, increasing your social skills as well.

- ▸ Spend part of your lunch break walking - Whether you work from home or go into an office, spending part of your lunch break walking helps you reset and clear your mind for the second half of the day.

It doesn't take much to add exercise to your routine. Just getting your body moving a few times a week can have astounding benefits. While speed is not a factor in getting those steps in, the faster you walk, the more you work those bodily systems, and the more calories you will burn.

50 percent of the benefit of the exercise is hearing and feeling your heart rate, your sweat and the pain levels that need to be encountered.

—Kevin R. Stone

The Rubber Band Effect

Senior executives and successful consultants who put in long days on the job, know that to have the energy levels needed to be just as effective at the end of the day as they are at the beginning, they have to incorporate an exercise program. When you get into motion, you tend to stay that way, and momentum will help you more easily top off when you hit a lull. That is much easier than having to start from zero each time.

I call this the rubber band effect. As you expend energy in physical activity, you create energy. Some of that is stored and able to be used later. It is akin to charging your batteries through activity, keeping the rubber band tight allows you to be more alert and effective.

> *Success is dependent upon the glands - sweat glands.*
>
> —*Zig Ziglar*

At the End of the Day, It Is Up to You

We all know the benefits of exercise, regardless of the amount you do. Making excuses for not doing it, as I sometimes do, or avoiding it entirely, can have a negative impact on your longevity. However, we can all get a little bit of physical activity. Not only does it benefit your body, but it is also good for your mind and spirit, too.

Here are some exercises to help you get moving

▶ Walk more
  ▷ Park further away from the store
  ▷ Tour your neighborhood on foot
  ▷ Take public transportation

▶ Quicken your walking pace

▶ Have a personal trainer create an exercise programs for you

▶ Take an exercise class

▶ Exercise with an exercise video or application

▶ What is one of your long-term fitness goals (I.e., doing a 5k, triathlon or participating in martial arts tournament)
  ▷ What do you need to do to achieve that fitness goal?

▶ Log your exercise for a month
  ▷ Are you happy with those results?

▶ How can you incrementally up your physical activity?

Get your free companion workbook for additional support at https://www.synergypersonaldevelopment.com/workbook/

Set Your Course

All through this book the focus has been on the realization that you are a person worth loving and fighting for. Those things do not come from external sources, they are inside of you. Being able to smile at that face in the mirror every morning and developing personal accountability to do your best each day will make you more confident and in control of your life. Inner confidence and a deep commitment to yourself are the keys to managing your stress, anxiety or depression. It is also important to find pockets where you are positive every day. Little by little, that positivity will grow.

Being a winner means having confidence in yourself while also being humble and appreciative of the people and opportunities in your life. Balancing confidence and humility isn't easy, but it does provide a solid foundation on which to build a life. The combination of these traits allows you to develop relationships focused on win-win situations and positive transformation. It also brings into view a realization that you have a great purpose in life. Your life is meant to be more than acquiescing to the needs and demands of others. Be good to yourself first. Then you will find the ability to be good to others in a more authentic way.

Although you've finished the book, it would be a good idea to continue to apply the exercises as a means of creating and maintaining a balanced life. Whether you need to work on yourself, your emotions, your environment, steps to move yourself into a more positive life or your daily habits these sections and chapters can provide new insights with every reading.

Set yourself a plan, put in the work and like going to the gym or developing any new skill, you will see progress slowly and first and in large swaths as you evaluate where you started and what you've achieved over a few days, weeks and months. Set large, seemingly unachievable goals for what you want to do in your life and keep progressing towards those dreams. It's the only way you will get there, winning one day at a time.

Acknowledgements

*T*here are so many people that helped to make this book possible. If I've forgotten anyone, my apologies.

Thanks to Mary Beth Thomas-Cooper who told me more than ten years ago that I had a book inside of me. This book started as *No Meds Required, How I Win My Battles With Depression*. My executive coach, JB Glossinger told me to write a book when I was out of work due to COVID and that got my mind turning on how to achieve this project. Then Resty Irial served as my sounding board for book topics sparking me to do this one.

There have been many folks who helped with editing, but my main support came from Hazel Pardinas-Kennedy who aided my journey to becoming a better writer with every chapter. I remember when Hazel first approached me. She said, "I like your ideas, but your grammar needs some help." To my friend Analee Advento, who motivated me to sit down and write at the times I would have rather been doing something else.

Towards the end of the process for creating the first draft, and crucial to editing the second draft was Chris Butchino, whose tough but fair feedback improved the depth of the content, David Clark and Alan Smollen who suggested a supplemental workbook, which you can get for free on my website. There were other editors too, Jade Lee and Dave Ludvik both helped turn my ideas into stories that first appeared on Medium.

Speaking of Medium, Dr. Mehmet Yildiz gave me a place to post these stories in his ILLUMINATION Integrated Publications. You can find early versions of every chapter and my road to self-publishing there. Writers and editors from the Illumination family: Liam Ireland inspired my not only to write but to aid others in their writing journeys, Terry Mansfield, Tree Langdon and Dr. Preeti Singh increased my belief that I was on the right path. As I was writing, my enthusiasm grew from all of the people that read, commented and followed me. I am humbled that you took the time to read my writing.

Thanks to my kids, James and Ayn who saw more than a dysfunctional dad in me. I hope that you have the opportunities to live the lives of your dreams. My Aunt, Suzi Pixley tried many of the techniques suggested in this book, validating they are actually beneficial. Jerry Kuhn, a mental wellness counselor, also corroborated that what has worked for me also works for others. To my mom, Sheri Cunningham who shared my writing with the rest of my family in California. Sometimes Japan seems far away and other times it's like we are just a few cities away.

And to my Guinea pigs in the Sunday morning English class: Shizuko Goshi, Kuniko Yoshida, Etsuzo Shigemoto, Naomasa Matake, Masako Tsuchia, Hirotaka Nakano and Soichiro Mori who test read every chapter to make sure they were easy to comprehend and appropriately focused. You guys are awesome.

While I was considering how to start this book, I was struck by the idea of comparing life's challenges to rock climbing. Marc Oxoby, Joyce Slaughter and Kim Haskitt found friends to contribute. The stories that Richard Schori, Sue Stekle and Maria Stadniuk provided made the opening of this book so powerful.

Thanks also to Kris Esplin who took the photo for the back cover, and Gregory Maidman who accepted the challenge of doing the final edits. Tami Boyce, thanks for your designs, you've made this book one that prospective readers would pick up, even though they'd never heard of me.

As I said in the dedication, I would like to also thank you for reading this book. I hope that it provides an example that with determination, a commitment to yourself and a supportive community you can achieve a life worth living each and every day. Win the day, and you can win your tomorrows, too.

About the Author

*J*ohn Cunningham has long felt the effects of stress, depression and anxiety. These challenges led him to a path of continual development and achievement as a means to find the light at the end of the tunnel. As a first-year university student, he worked at San Jose State University's radio station, KSJS to help transition into college life. There he found several life-long friendships and a level of popularity as an on-air personality. This made his transition into adulthood an easier one.

After finishing his degree, John trained in the martial arts, earning a black belt in Tae Kwon Do while studying under Black Belt Hall of Fame Members Grand Master Jim L. Buhisan and his brother Grand Master Bo Buhisan at USA Martial Arts. His purpose in studying was to defeat a life-long anxiety focused on quitting before reaching his goals which hindered his ability to make significant achievements. He now carries that black belt mentality with him wherever he goes.

In 1998 John moved to Japan and became an English teacher. This helped him to develop the coaching and mentoring skills he uses to this day in helping others get more out of life and achieve both their personal and professional goals.

John has had many encounters with depression and has committed himself to finding solutions that do not rely on medications. Instead, he focuses on self-love, emotional intelligence, setting and achieving goals and finding ways to incorporate more positivity into life every day. This led him to explore creative outlets for enriching his life and benefiting others as well. In the early 2000s he created *Relaxation Media* with long-time friend Sean Frame. This video podcast was helpful in reducing stress and anxiety for thousands of people through short nature videos mixed with calming background music. The podcast became the #1 self-help video podcast in iTunes worldwide and had several thousand downloads of every episode by the time production ended.

In 2020 John took to writing on Medium.com in an effort to tie his experience in training with his techniques for coping with mental distress. His personal development articles there have been called inspiring and motivational. He is considered an expert on personal development to many of his readers and followers.

John now has his own coaching and mentoring practice, based in Tokyo, Japan. He serves clients all over the world. You can find out more about his services at https://www.synergypersonaldevelopment.com.

CPSIA information can be obtained
at www.ICGtesting.com
Printed in the USA
BVHW030239261021
619844BV00006B/265